**FITZWARREN PUBLISHING**

# THE LICENSING HANDBOOK

*A Guide to Obtaining a Licence
and Running Licensed Premises*

Liz Gwinnell

FHB

© Fitzwarren Publishing 1997

ISBN 0 9524812 51

*Published by*
Fitzwarren Publishing,
PO Box 6887,
Highgate,
London N19 2TR

A CIP record for this book is available from the British Library

All rights reserved. No part of this publication may be reproduced in any material form (including photocopying or storing it in any medium by electronic means and whether or not transiently or incidentally to some other use of this publication) without the written permission of the copyright owner except in accordance with the Copyright, Designs and Patents Act 1988 or under the terms of a licence issued by the Copyright Licensing Agency Limited, 90 Tottenham Court Road, London, W1P 9HE, England. Applications for the copyright owner's written permission to reproduce any part of this publication should be addressed to the publisher.

Warning: The doing of an unauthorised act in relation to a copyright work may result in both a civil claim for damages and criminal prosecution.

Printed and bound by UTL Ltd, London W1

Liz Gwinnell is a legal executive and freelance writer

# CONTENTS

Contents

Preface

1. **A Brief History of Licensing**
   10.

2. **Introduction: The Basics of Licensing**
   Justices' Licences - Who needs one? 14; Licensing Justices 14; Justices Licences - What are they? 15; Sales of Intoxicating Liquor 15; On and off licences 15; Restaurants 16; Hotels 16; Restrictions on granting a justices licence - premises 16; Restrictions on granting a licence - persons 17; Children 17; Employees 18; Licensing hours 19; Restrictions on licensing hours 19; Drinking up time 19; Register of Justices' licences 19; Notices 20.

3. **Applying for a New On or Off Licence**
   Preliminary matters 21; The Clerk to the Justices 21; The Chief Officer of Police 22; Proper Officers 22; The Fire Authority 22; The Letter to be Sent with the Application 23; The Hearing 24; Case history 25.

4. **Protection Orders and Transferring Licences**
   Protection Orders 31; The Hearing 32; Transferring a Licence from One Person to Another 33; The Hearing 35; Transferring a licence from One Set of Premises to Another 36; Ordinary and special removals 36; Applying for Removals 37.

5. **Varying Licences**
   Applications for Variations 38; Variations to Permitted Licensing Hours 38; General Orders of Exemption 38; Special Orders of Exemption 39; Supper Hours and

# THE LICENSING HANDBOOK

Restaurant Certificates 39; Application for Supper Hours or Restaurant Certificate 40; Application for a Special Hours Certificate 41; Extended Hours Orders 42; Restrictions on Permitted Licensing Hours 43; Seasonal and Early Closing Licences 44; Displaying notices 44.

## 6. Occasional Licences and Permissions
Occasional Licences 45; Occasional Permissions 46; Application for an Occasional Permission 46.

## 7. Renewing a Justices' Licence
The Need to Renew a Licence 48; Forfeiture and Revocation 49; Surrendering a Justices' Licence 50; Licences in Suspense 51.

## 8. Restaurant licensing
Part IV Licences 52; Application for Restaurant and Similar Licences 53; Disqualifications and Prohibitions 53; Displaying a Notice 54; Case histories 54.

## 9. Clubs
Introduction 56; Registration Certificates: Prerequisites 56; Application for a Registration Certificate 57; Objections 58; Procedure 60; Registration Certificates in General 61; Permitted Hours 64; Supper Hours and Restaurant certificates 64; Special hours certificates 64; Conditions on Special Hours Certificates 65; Extended Hours Orders 65; Extending Nightclubs' Hours 66.

## 10. The Licensing of Marriage Venues
Approval of Venues for Civil Marriages 68; The Application for a Marriage Licence 68; The Registrars 70; Religious Connections 70; Conditions 71; Notices 71; The Room 72; Renewal 72; Revocation 72; Reviews 73; Records 73; Case Histories 73.

# CONTENTS

**11. Public Entertainment and Copyright Music Licences**
Public Entertainment Licences 75; Case Histories 76; Copyright Music 76; The Tariffs 77; Phonographic Performance Licences 78.

**12. Betting Office Licences**
Introduction 80; Bookmakers' Permits 80; Betting Agency Permits 80; Applying for a Betting Office Licence 81; Notices 81; Refusal of a Betting Office Licence 82; Renewing a Betting Office Licence 84; Death of a Licence Holder 85.

**13. Gaming**
Gaming 86; Application 86; Consent by the Gaming Board 87; Applying for a Gaming Licence 88; Notices 88; The Licence 89; Refusing to Grant a Licence 90; Restrictions 91; Appeals 92; Renewal 93; Revocation of a Certificate of Consent 93; Cancellation 94; Convictions 95; Disqualification Orders 96; Death of a Licence Holder 97; Transferring a Gaming Licence 97; Refusing a Transfer 98; Gaming Licence Fees 98; Companies Holding Gaming Licences 99; Relinquishing a Gaming Licence 99; Fruit Machine Licences 99; Bingo Licences 100.

**14. Gaming Licences - Members' Clubs**
Registration 101; Refusal 101; Restrictions on Registration 102; Appeals 102; Cancellation of Registration 103; Registration Certificates 104; Relinquishing Registration 104; Restrictions on Games Played 104.

**15. Legal rights in restaurants**
Introduction 106; The Food 106; "Waiter, there's a Fly in my Soup" 107; The Police 107; "There's a Rat in the Kitchen..." 108; Bookings and reservations 108.

# THE LICENSING HANDBOOK

**16. Forms**
    1. Application for a Justices' Licence 110; 2. Certificate of Service 110; 3. Newspaper notice 111; 4. Application for a Protection Order 112; 5. Application to Transfer a Justices' Licence 112; 6. Application for a Supper Hours/Restaurant Certificate (Licensed Premises) 114; 7. Application for a Special Hours Certificate 115; 8. Application for an Occasional Licence/Special Order of Exemption 116; 9. Application for a Betting Office Licence 117; 10. Application for the Renewal of a Betting Office Licence 117; 11. Application for a bingo licence 118.

**17. Glossary**
    120.

**Further reading**
    Statutes 122; Legal Textbooks 122; Other Helpful Publications 123.

**Index**
    124.

# PREFACE

Licensing is an extensive subject and not just concerned with the sale of alcohol. For the sake of practicality (and sanity) this book confines itself to areas which concern our everyday lives. It is intended as a clear and practical guide through what can sometimes seem a hostile and bureaucratic jungle but, as in any area of law, legal advice should be sought before embarking on more complex matters.

The law is often conceived to be a dusty and complicated subject, filled with traps for the unwary and written in tedious and archaic language. It is however a fascinating, relevant to everyone and shouldn't be the sole preserve of lawyers. In writing this guide, I attempt to explain things as clearly as possible without trying to impress the reader with my legal vocabulary.

I have adopted the Fitzwarren house style of referring to the unspecified person in the masculine.

I would like to add a word of caution about the book's coverage. It deals with a complex area of law. The leading textbook runs to over 2,000 pages. Inevitably this work is a very condensed version. That and the fact that laws frequently change mean the reader would be well advised to treat this book as merely a starting point, and if there is any doubt or ambiguity about what is said a more definitive source of law or better still a solicitor should be consulted.

I would like to express my thanks to the following for their help and support, Kennet Licensing Division, David Nolder & Co solicitors, Wiltshire County Council, Kennet District Council, Oscars Nightclub, Longleat, the Swan Hotel, Bradford on Avon, the Stakis Hotel, Bath.

The book covers the law as it stands in England. Except for different and much stricter rules about Sunday licensing this law is the same in Wales. (Monmouth adopts Welsh mores for this purpose). Scotland, Northern Ireland and other parts of the British Isles have substantially different laws and procedures.

I believe that I state the law as of 1 March 1997.

# 1. A BRIEF HISTORY OF LICENSING

Drinking in inns, taverns and alehouses is a centuries old tradition, a colourful thread running through the fabric of our social history. The consumption of alcohol and the company and conversation which usually accompanies it has an appeal regardless of social class, geographical location or education. A look at the history of our public houses provides a cameo of the way our ancestors lived and reflects the social and economic conditions prevailing at those times.

Inns were a welcome respite for ostlers and travellers alike in the days when transport was horse drawn and roads barely more than muddy tracks. In addition they were an important centre for the exchange of news and information when communications were poor. Inns were often a favourite haunt of the highwayman, and on the other side of the law, frequently hosted coroners' courts. They were also places where businessmen met to execute conveyances or seek legal counsel. Mary Queen of Scots was even imprisoned in one.

The appeal of good food and wine in a cosy atmosphere on a cold winter's night spurred many philosophical, scientific and literary institutions into existence as well as providing a place where the every day troubles and toils of life could be forgotten. Inns inspired many a writer to include atmospheric descriptions of the life and characters within them - William Shakespeare and Charles Dickens to name but two - in their books; whilst the names of many public houses still preserve some remnant of days gone by with their allusions to heraldic emblems and political affiliations.

It was as a result of the nation's propensity for tippling that the first major licensing law was passed in 1552. This effectively passed control of the licensing trade to the Government who had become increasingly alarmed at the widespread consumption of alcohol across the country. The Act was passed chiefly to control the growth of the alehouse which, by all accounts, attracted the less desirable elements of society who frequently ended up on the wrong side of the law after a drinking session.

# 1. A BRIEF HISTORY OF LICENSING

44   During the reign of James I four licensing enactments were passed with each one becoming more and more stringent in its effect. Anyone convicted of drunkenness was also treated harshly - a fine of five shillings or a stint of six hours in the stocks.

In 1627 anyone keeping an alehouse without a licence had to forfeit twenty-one shillings or be whipped in default of payment. A second conviction for the same offence was punishable by a sentence of one month in a House of Correction. This was how seriously the Government viewed the drinking problem.

Drinking was by no means confined to the poorer elements of society. At the higher end of the social scale, no gentleman would ever leave the table of his host sober in case this was seen as a slight on his hospitality.

In the seventeenth century the use of distilled spirits began to spread across Europe and at the outbreak of the English Civil War, in 1643, Parliament imposed excise duties on ale, beer, cider and perry. These duties remained in force after the Restoration and by 1692 the duty on a barrel of strong beer was five shillings. The public naturally began to look elsewhere to satisfy their thirst. To spite the French, Parliament prohibited the importation of brandy and other foreign spirits and sought to encourage home industries by allowing everyone who paid a small duty to distil and retail spirits made from English corn. It was hardly surprising that the taste for gin soon reached outlandish proportions, so that by 1736 one house in every four in London was a ginshop. Alarmed at this spiralling excess, the Government decided to implement restrictive legislation and on 29 September 1736 the Gin Act came into force.

This Act levied a tax of twenty shillings on every gallon of gin sold and required every person who sold it to be licensed. The fee for such a licence was £50. Anyone found selling gin without a licence would be fined £100. Anticipating that this would prove to be a highly unpopular measure, a double guard was mounted at Kensington Palace that morning and a detachment of Guards sent to Covent Garden to dispel any dissenting crowds.

Rather than squeezing out the illicit retailers who sold from wheelbarrows, sheds and any other suitable premises, however the distillers simply took out wine licences and sold concoctions of gin, sugar and spice under the name of wine. Hawkers sold it in the streets and men posing as chemists opened shops and sold gin in physic bottles as a medicine. In the taverns and alehouses it was simply sold under a different name such as "Ladies' Delight" or "Make Shift."

The consumption of gin in England and Wales continued to rise and between 1733 and 1742 rose from 11 million to 20 million gallons per year. Attempting once more to gain control of the situation, in 1743 the Government abolished the duty levied on gin and reduced the £50 licence fee to twenty shillings. Furthermore, licences were only to be granted to those who kept public victualling houses, inns, coffee houses, alehouses or brandy shops and to no other trades whatsoever.

Gin continued to be the principal tipple of Londoners however and in 1751 further legislation prohibited distillers of gin to sell it either by retail or to unlicensed publicans.

During the following century, the Alehouse Act of 1828 required alehouses, inns and victualling houses to obtain justices' licences before they could sell any kind of excisable liquor. As a privilege, ale-house keepers were allowed to keep a billiards table for public use on the premises.

The Beer Act which followed in 1830 allowed any householder whose name was on the rate book (with the exception of Sheriff's officers) to sell beer, by retail, without a licence on payment of a fee of two guineas. No other intoxicating liquor could be sold. Beer could be sold from a person's dwelling house whether it was to be consumed on or off the premises but such licences were usually subject to certain penalties. Within three months, 25,000 people had paid the requisite two guineas and during the century beer houses multiplied with many also selling gin and other spirits.

In 1834 off licences were granted for the sale of beer to be consumed away from the premises and in 1860 licences were granted to wine and refreshment houses. In 1869 wine and beer houses were brought under magisterial control and in 1872 public houses were no longer allowed to keep their doors open all night. By a further Act of 1869 licences granted under the 1830 Beer Act were not to be

# 1. A BRIEF HISTORY OF LICENSING

renewed without a certificate first being obtained from the Justices assembled at a General Licensing Meeting.

Thus were the foundations laid for the reforms of the twentieth century as the law responded to the development of society and modern day living.

Public houses and restaurants are today subject to stringent legal requirements and whilst the establishments themselves and the drinks they offer have perhaps become more refined, drinking and eating still has the appeal that it had all those centuries ago.

## 2. INTRODUCTION: THE BASICS OF LICENSING

### Justices' Licences - Who Needs One?

Anyone who wishes to sell, by retail, intoxicating liquor needs a justices' licence. Failure to comply with this requirement constitutes a breach of section 160 of the Licensing Act 1964 which can result in severe penalties.

### Licensing Justices

Justices' licences are granted by licensing justices who are a body of magistrates empowered to deal with licensing matters for a defined geographical area. The licensing justices hold General Annual Licensing Meetings (also known as *Brewster sessions*) in February of each year and four licensing sessions, known as *transfer sessions*, are held at regular intervals throughout the twelve month period. Most types of licensing application can be made at the transfer sessions but some, for example, renewal of justices' licences, must be made at the Brewster Sessions. The date of the annual Brewster Sessions and subsequent transfer sessions are advertised in advance in the local press and notified to the Police and holders of justices' licences.

Once granted, a justices' licence will be effective until the date printed on the licence and, if it is not revoked or forfeited within that time, is then renewed by the licensing justices at the appropriate Brewster sessions.

# 2. INTRODUCTION: THE BASICS OF LICENSING

## Justices' Licences - What are they?

Justices' licences' can take several forms. The two main types for public houses and premises wishing to sell intoxicating liquor by retail (supermarkets for example) are the on and off licence respectively. Variations of these can then be granted to cover events, such as when a person wishes to sell intoxicating liquor at some place other than the premises at which he is licensed to do so.

The first thing to do before embarking on any licensing application of whatever nature is to find out which licensing division has jurisdiction for the area. Usually a telephone call to the local magistrates' court will answer this question and it will then be to this division that all applications and queries are made.

## Sales of Intoxicating Liquor

The key words in the Licensing Act 1964 are *intoxicating liquor* and *sale by retail*.

A sale by retail is the sale of intoxicating liquor at any one time to any person.

Intoxicating liquor means spirits, wine, beer, cider and any other fermented, distilled or spirituous liquor with the exception of perfumes, spirits or wines intended for medicinal purposes rather than as a beverage; certain recognised flavouring essences and any liquor not exceeding 0.5% proof at the time of the sale.

## On and Off Licences

These are the two main types of justices' licence applicable to public houses and other places where intoxicating liquor is sold by retail. An off licence permits the retail sale of intoxicating liquor where it is to be consumed off the premises. Off licences can either be granted for the sale of intoxicating liquor of all descriptions or limited to the sale of beer, cider and wine only.

# THE LICENSING HANDBOOK

On licences are usually granted for the retail sale of intoxicating liquor of all descriptions but can also be granted for the sale of beer, cider and wine only; beer and cider only; or cider only or wine only. An on licence usually allows a sale by retail for consumption either on or off the premises although certain conditions may be attached to it which can, for example, permit purchased alcohol to be consumed on the premises only.

## Restaurants

Where a restaurant wishes to sell intoxicating liquor to diners, a special justices' licence must be obtained. These licences are known as "Part IV" licences and cover the situation where alcoholic beverages are served with meals. Where a restaurant has a bar which is intended to be used by members of the general public as well as diners, a full justices on licence should be obtained.

## Hotels

If a hotel has a bar which is open to both non-residents and residents it will need to obtain a full justices on licence. This will then cover the sale and provision of alcohol to those eating meals in the restaurant and those drinking in the bar. If a hotel only has a dining room then it will need to obtain a restaurant and/or combined restaurant and residential licence to permit it to sell drinks with the meals it serves.

## Restrictions on Granting a Justices' Licence: Premises

Premises which are situated on land acquired or appropriated for special road building schemes, such as motorways, are automatically disqualified from receiving a justices' licence. Automatic disqualification also applies to premises which are primarily used as

## 2. INTRODUCTION: THE BASICS OF LICENSING

a garage unless a licence was granted to those premises before 22 August 1988 and the licence has not lapsed since then. Garages can be granted off licences, however where their primary use is for something other than the sale of petrol. If, for example, it sold petrol but its sales of food or other items regularly exceeded its sales of petrol, the premises would not be considered to be primarily used as a garage.

### Restrictions on Granting a Justices' Licence: Persons

Certain categories of person are automatically disqualified from obtaining a justices licence. These include Sheriff's officers and any officer executing the legal process of any Court. Convictions for various offences including forging or using a justices licence knowing it to be forged, allowing premises for which a licence was held to be used as a brothel, selling liquor or exposing it for sale by retail without a justices' licence or selling it or exposing it for sale at a place other than that authorised by a justices licence, may also lead to disqualification. A second conviction for one of these latter offences will result in a person not being able to hold a justices' licence for a period of five years and for a third or subsequent offence, a person may be disqualified for a longer period or even for life.

### Children

A holder of a justices' licence must not allow children under fourteen to be in a licensed bar during permitted licensing hours. The exception to the rule is where such a child is the child of the licensee or resides at the premises or is in the bar for the sole purpose of getting to another part of the building where there is no alternative route.

Children under fourteen years of age are allowed to be in a bar where they are accompanied by a person who is eighteen years or over and where those premises are covered by a children's certificate.

A licence holder or someone employed by him must not sell intoxicating liquor to a person under eighteen years of age or knowingly allow such a person to consume intoxicating liquor in a bar. A person under the age of eighteen also commits an offence where he either buys, attempts to buy or consumes intoxicating liquor in a bar.

A person aged sixteen years or over may buy beer, cider, perry or porter for consumption with a meal where that meal is to be taken in an area set aside for such purposes and which is not a bar. A bar is any place used exclusively or mostly for the sale or consumption of intoxicating liquor.

## Employees

No staff under the age of eighteen can be employed in any bar of licensed premises when the bar is open for the sale and consumption of alcoholic beverages. Even if a person does not receive a wage from an employer he will still be considered an employee in the eyes of the law. However a person will not be considered to be an employee when he is in the bar in the course of his employment to pass on or receive a message or where he is coming from another area of the establishment where he works which is not a bar and where there is no alternative route.

## Licensing Hours

Licensing hours are now governed by the Licensing (Sunday Hours) Act 1995 and the Licensing Acts of 1964 and 1988. It is an offence to sell intoxicating liquor outside the permitted hours unless an extension has been granted.

For an on licence the permitted hours are:
- Weekdays: 11.00am - 11.00pm

## 2. INTRODUCTION: THE BASICS OF LICENSING

- Sundays and Good Friday: noon - 10.30pm
- Christmas Day: noon - 3.00pm and 7.00pm - 10.30pm

For an off licences the permitted hours are:
- Weekdays: 8.00am - 11.00pm
- Sundays: 10.00am - 10.30pm
- Christmas Day: noon - 3.00pm and 7.00pm - 10.30pm
- Good Friday 8.00am - 10.30pm

For on licences and weekdays other than Christmas Day or Good Friday the licensing hours may commence at 10.00am where the licensing justices are satisfied that the requirements of the licensing district are such that drinking hours should commence one hour earlier than usual.

### Restrictions on Licensing Hours

When an on licence is granted, restrictions may be imposed on the hours permitted by law. Such restrictions, however can only be applied for by a chief officer of Police or by or on behalf of a person living or carrying on business or in charge of an educational establishment in the neighbourhood where the licensing justices feel it desirable to avoid or reduce disturbances to those persons.

### Drinking Up Time

Drinking up time is twenty minutes after *time* is called in a public house or thirty minutes where customers are eating a meal at the premises and the intoxicating liquor is supplied as an ancillary to the meal.

# THE LICENSING HANDBOOK

## Register of Justices' Licences

The clerk to the licensing justices in each area keeps a register detailing:

- the justices' licences granted in the district;
- information about the licensed premises;
- who owns the premises;
- the name(s) of the licence holder(s).

Additional information is then added as is appropriate such as details of any convictions made against licence holders, acts of forfeiture or disqualification and any other matters considered relevant.

## Notices

A holder of a justices' licence must keep painted or affixed to the licensed premises and in an obvious place (traditionally over the front door) a notice detailing his name and after his name, the word "licensed" followed by words sufficient to express the business for which the licence is granted. Such words must state whether the licence is an on or off licence and if appropriate, whether it is a six day or early closing licence. The licence holder must not indicate by any means whatsoever that he is authorised to sell types of liquor that he is not authorised to sell.

Club premises do not need to display such a notice where the licensing justices relieve them of such a requirement. A holder of a residential licence is also exempt and the requirement is also modified for the holder of a residential or combined restaurant and residential licence.

# 3. APPLYING FOR A NEW ON LICENCE

## Preliminary Matters

Application for a new licence is made at the transfer sessions held at the local magistrates' court. A list of the date of future transfer sessions is published regularly in the local paper or the licensing justices department of the magistrates' court will provide details.

Before applying for a justices' licence it is always worth telephoning the licensing justices department to check on what documents are required, as procedure can varies from court to court. The court will also be able to provide the names and addresses of the local fire authority and appropriate Police station for inclusion in the application.

Generally, the application must contain the applicant's full name and address, his occupation during the last six months, the name and address of the premises to be licensed and the type of licence being applied for. The application form must be signed and dated (see *Form 1* on page 110).

Once the application form has been completed, copies should be sent to the authorities discussed in the sections below at least twenty-one days in advance of the hearing date. Sending copy applications in this way is known as *serving*.

## The Clerk to the Justices

The original application and a copy of it should be sent to the clerk to the justices at the magistrates' court with licensing jurisdiction for the area in which the premises are situated. These should be sent with a cheque for £12.50 made out to *The Clerk to the Justices*. A plan of the premises should be sent. The Licensing Acts do not specify any particular form that the plan must take or whether it should be professionally drawn. Justices however may have their own requirements some, for example, require the areas in which alcohol is to be sold to be coloured with a particular colour and other areas such as the kitchen, toilets, to be marked in a contrasting colour. It is therefore advisable to check with the court beforehand.

## The Chief Officer of Police

Where the premises are in the City of London, a copy of the application should be sent to the Commissioner of Police for the City. Where the premises are in the Metropolitan Police District it should be sent to the Commissioner of Police of the Metropolis. In other areas, it should be sent to the Chief Constable. Often the licensing justices department, who will be familiar with the names of the Police officers dealing with licensing matters and will be able to supply a contact name at the relevant Police station.

## Proper Officers

A copy of the application should be sent to the proper officers of the district and parish councils where the premises to be licensed are outside London and to the proper officer of the community council where they are within a community. For premises inside Greater London, a copy must also be sent to the proper office of the local authority who is the clerk to the relevant borough council or the clerk to the common council.

## The Fire Authority

A telephone call to the district council will identify the fire authority for an area.

# 3. APPLYING FOR A NEW LICENCE

## The Letter to be Sent with the Application

A letter should be sent with each application setting out the intention to apply for a justices' licence and asking the party concerned to acknowledge safe receipt and confirm that they have no objections to the licence being granted.

Someone who has not held a justices' licence before, should in his letter to the Police, give details of any licensing experience he has, convictions (including any for driving), date of birth and occupation for the past year. Additionally, references should be supplied from reliable sources such as the family doctor or solicitor testifying to good character. This will save time later as the Police frequently request such information from applicants who have not previously held a justices' licence. The justices are also keen to see such references as they will want to satisfy themselves that they are granting a licence to a person who is a fit and proper person to hold a justices' licence.

The notices should then be sent by first class registered post (for a signature on delivery) which is usually sufficient proof that they have been served. A certificate of service should also be prepared which lists the names and addresses of those who have been sent copy applications which is then given to the Court on the day of the hearing (see *Form 2* on page 110).

It is important to note that when calculating the twenty-one days for service, the day of posting, the day the application is received by the other party and the day of the hearing itself do not count as notice days.

After the applications have been sent notice of the application must be displayed for seven days on or near the premises which are to be licensed where it can easily be read by members of the public. This must be done not more than twenty-eight days before the hearing date. Notice of the application must also be advertised in the public notices section of a newspaper circulating in the area in which the premises to be licensed are situated. This need not necessarily be a local paper but the advertisement must be published between twenty-eight and fourteen days in advance of the hearing date (see *Form 3* on page 111).

Each of the recipients should confirm in writing that they have no objections to the licence being granted. If they do have any objections, they may attend the hearing to voice them.

Justices often wish to inspect premises in advance of the hearing as a licence may not be granted unless the justices are satisfied that the premises are structurally suitable for the class of licence required.

## The Hearing

An applicant can attend the hearing on his own or instruct a solicitor to represent him. However no great legal skills are required and there is no reason why representation should be necessary.

On arrival at court the applicant should make himself known to the usher, who will then say which court room the hearing will be in. The applicant should then take a seat at the back along with the other applicants.

As the justices enter everyone in the room stands up and the clerk calls the first matter before the justices. Applicants are asked to give a brief background to their application matter, identifying the premises and their relationship to it. They will then be asked to take oath and answer the questions put by the justices. Any objectors present may then cross examine and may also produce witnesses to give evidence on oath. Objectors need give no notice to the justices before the hearing that they intend to object and so their presence may come as something of a surprise. If there are objectors present, it is important to keep calm and answer any questions honestly and clearly.

If it is the police who are objecting however, then they will notify the applicant of their objections in advance of the hearing. The police often object as a way of voicing their concerns over licensing premises in a residential area.

The justices have a general discretion to grant a licence to anyone whom they consider to be a fit and proper person to hold a justices' licence. They can also attach conditions to a licence where they feel that to do so is in the public interest or for any other reason they consider necessary. Where a supermarket, for example, is applying

# 3. APPLYING FOR A NEW LICENCE

to start selling alcoholic beverages, a condition of the licence might be that the area in which the liquor is to be sold is to be segregated from the rest of the premises. For a hotel, a condition may be attached to the licence prohibiting off licence sales. An applicant who applies for a licence for a public house will apply for a licence to sell intoxicating liquor of all descriptions either on or off the premises and if the justices only wish it to sell liquor to be consumed on the premises a condition will be attached to reflect this.

When granting off licences, the justices have no power to attach conditions but may instead require a party to give undertakings. Whilst non-compliance with an undertaking to, for example, only sell certain types of liquor will not lead to prosecution, it can result in any application to renew the licence at a future date being refused.

For breach of conditions attached to on licences the position is more serious in that prosecution may follow as well as a refusal to renew the licence at a future application and may result in the licence being revoked.

Undertakings may also be required of on licence applicants where attaching a condition to a licence is not considered appropriate. This might be the case where work has been recommended to be carried out by the fire brigade and an undertaking given by the applicant to have it completed within a certain period of time.

Once the application has been heard the justices will decide immediately whether or not the licence is granted. If objectors are present the licensing justices will consider whether they should pay the applicant's costs (if he has incurred any) or, if he having been unsuccessful in his application, whether he should pay theirs. If the Police are the unsuccessful objectors they are usually excluded from paying the applicant's costs so long as they have acted properly.

## Case History: Singh's Grocery Shop

Peter Singh owns a local corner shop which opens seven days a week from 7am to 9pm. He now wishes to sell alcohol from the premises and applies to the local magistrates' court for an off licence permitting him to do so.

He discovers that there are two types of off licence he can apply for - either one to sell alcoholic beverages of all description or one limiting alcohol sold to beer, wine and cider. As he wishes to sell a range of goods from brandy to beer he decides to apply for the former.

He completes the application form and sends it to the Police, justices' clerk, local authority and fire authority and is notified by the magistrates' court that his application will be considered on 1 March. On the morning of the hearing he arrives at court and takes a seat at the back as indicated by the usher. However when his application comes before the magistrates it transpires that he did not advertise his intention to apply for an off licence in the newspaper. The magistrates confer and agree to postpone the matter.

Peter then makes a fresh application to the magistrates including the next transfer session date and sends another copy to all the relevant parties. He changes the date on the notice displayed in his shop window and places an advert in the public notices section of the local newspaper.

That evening, Mr Mulhoony, a Methodist Minister, returns from an extended trip to Ireland. On his way home from the railway station he buys a copy of the local evening paper and sees notice of Peter's application for an off licence. Mr Mulhoony is a tee totaller who does not see why a corner shop needs to sell alcohol when there is an off licence nearby and three public houses in the area.

That evening the owner of the Regal Off Licence, two streets away from Peter Singh's shop, also sees the notice advising of the off licence application in the local paper. He becomes concerned that if it is granted his own business will suffer.

The next morning Mr Mulhoony telephones the local Council to protest about the off licence application. He is told to ring the licensing department at Blenheim Magistrates' Court and does so. He is told by the clerk that applications for off licences are heard at transfer sessions in front of three magistrates responsible for licensing matters. She also tells him that the next transfer session is scheduled for 17 April. Mr Mulhoony tells her that he objects most strongly to the application being made and is told that he can go to court and put his objections in person to the magistrates. He is told

# 3. APPLYING FOR A NEW LICENCE

that he can bring witnesses with him if he wishes, and that he does not need to notify the court in advance of his intention to make objections to the magistrates.

Later that day the manager of the Regal Off Licence also telephones the court and obtains the same information. Any member of the public, he is told, can oppose the granting of a new licence on public as well as private grounds or on the grounds that it will affect a person's trade or other interests.

About a week later Peter receives notification from the magistrates' clerk that his application is to be heard at 10.30am on 17 April. He draws up an outline plan of his shop detailing where he intends to put the alcoholic drink if he is granted the off licence. He thinks it would be best to have it behind the till and on high shelves so that only he and his staff can reach it.

On the day the application is to be heard, Peter attends the court at 10.30am and gives his name and the nature of his application to the court usher. He is then asked to take a seat at the back of Court One and does so. Several other applications are heard before the magistrates' clerk announces his application for an off licence. The clerk then asks if there are any objectors present and Peter is surprised to see two men put up their hands. The clerk asks them for their names and addresses and then asks Peter to come forward and take the witness stand. Peter does so and is asked to swear an oath and confirm his name and address. The magistrates then invite him to tell them about his application.

Peter explains that he has run his corner shop in Presley Road, Newtown for the past five years and now wishes to obtain an off licence to allow him to sell alcoholic beverages for consumption off the premises.

The magistrates ask him if he has ever held a justices' licence before and Peter replies that he has not. He is asked why he wishes to sell alcoholic beverages and he explains that he sells everything from cat food to curry powder and is open from 7am to 9pm. Customers are always asking why he doesn't sell bottles of wine or cans of beer as his shop is in the middle of a suburban area where people call in for provisions they forgot to buy in town or when other shops aren't open.

# THE LICENSING HANDBOOK

The justices ask him if he is familiar with the problem of selling alcohol to the underaged and Peter replies that he is. He says that if a licence were granted he would keep the alcohol on shelves behind the till where only he and his staff could reach it. He also says that these shelves are fitted with shutters which can be pulled down to hide the bottles during the times when sales of alcohol are not permitted by law.

He is asked if he is familiar with the laws about when he is allowed to sell alcohol and Peter replies that he knows he cannot sell it before 10am on Sundays and that on Christmas Day only between noon and 3pm and 7pm to 10.30pm. The magistrates' clerk then thanks Peter who steps down from the stand and resumes his seat.

The clerk then calls the first of the objectors, Mr Mulhoony. Mr Mulhoony is told that he may cross examine Mr Singh if he so wishes but Mr Mulhoony replies that he simply wishes to address the magistrates. He is then asked to swear an oath and to confirm his name and address. He does this and is then asked to outline his objections to the off licence being granted.

Mr Mulhoony says that he is objecting to the off licence being granted on the grounds that he is a Methodist minister who is strongly opposed to the way in which drink is available everywhere you turn these days. He feels it is the cause of many of the problems in society and causes nothing but trouble. He feels that it will only increase drinking in the neighbourhood and that even more empty cans and litter will be left in front gardens and on the streets.

When he has finished, the magistrates' clerk tells Mr Singh that he has the right to cross examine Mr Mulhoony about what he has said. Mr Singh declines to comment.

The magistrates thank Mr Mulhoony and he returns to his seat.

The clerk then calls the manager of the off licence who is asked to take the stand, swear an oath and confirm his name and address. He does so and identifies himself as the manager of the Regal Off Licence. He is told that he has the right to cross examine Mr Singh but he says he does not need to do that. Instead he addresses the magistrates and says that he wishes to object to the off licence being granted to Peter Singh on the grounds that it will affect his trade as their shops are only two streets apart. He feels that Peter has an

# 3. APPLYING FOR A NEW LICENCE

unfair advantage in that people go to his shop for groceries and newspapers and that if he sells alcohol as well they won't bother to walk to his shop for it anymore.

The magistrates ask him who his main customers are and he says that they are mainly from the housing estate nearby. They then ask him what his best selling lines are. He says that he has a large turnover of bottled cider and cans of lager. They ask him if any of the residents living near Peter Singh's shop are regular customers and he admits that the gangs of youngsters which hang around outside his shop in the precinct tend to put a lot of people off. Peter is told that he has a right to cross examine the manager but has no wish to do so.

The magistrates take a few moments to confer and then announce that the off licence is granted. They stress Peter's need to uphold the licensing laws in relation to permitted hours and underage drinking. They also state that alcohol in the shop must be kept behind the shutters during the hours when sales are not permitted by law and locked shut when the shop is closed. As it is an off licence that is being applied for, the magistrates have no power to attach this requirement as conditions to the licence but they ask Peter to give an undertaking instead. He is told that before giving an undertaking as any subsequent breach can result in the licence being revoked or the magistrates refusing to renew it at a later date. Peter confirms that he understands all this and gives the undertaking.

Mr Mulhoony is furious and when he gets home he telephones the clerk at the magistrates' court again to see if there is anything he can do to stop the licence being granted. He explains that he went to the application and put his objections to the magistrates but that the licence was granted in any event. He is told that as he attended the application in person as an objector he has a right to make an appeal against the grant of the off licence. The clerk says that he should write a letter informing the Crown Court of his wish to appeal against the magistrates' decision of 17 April to grant an off licence to Singh's and state his grounds for doing so. He is told that in some districts a person making an appeal is required to complete a standard form but that in this particular area, letters will be accepted as forming the basis of an appeal. The clerk tells Mr Mulhoony that his letter must reach him within twenty-one days and that he must send a copy of it to Peter Singh within the same period of time.

When the Court receive Mr Mulhoony's notice of appeal the clerk sends it on to the clerk at the Crown Court. He then notifies Peter Singh, who has received notice of the appeal, that the off licence remains in suspension until the appeal is over - that is, that he cannot start selling alcohol until the Crown Court either uphold or overturn the magistrates' decision.

About a week later Peter receives notification from the Crown Court that the appeal is to be heard on 26 June.

He attends Court on that date and discovers that the appeal is no more than a re-run of the application except that it takes place before different magistrates. At the end of the hearing the Crown Court uphold the magistrates' decision to grant the off licence. Peter's licence is to run from the date of the appeal.

# 4. PROTECTION ORDERS AND TRANSFERRING LICENCES

Where a justices' licence is in existence for a set of premises an application can be made to transfer it from the current to a new licensee. The fictional Moonrakers Wine Bar will be used to illustrate how this operates.

## Protection Orders

Harry Moonshine has held a justices' licence for Moonrakers for the past two years. However he now wishes to move to Scotland. If he is not at Moonrakers, the Wine Bar is without a licensee and if it sells intoxicating liquor will be in breach of the licensing laws. On the other hand it cannot jeopardise business by ceasing to trade. Barnaby, the bar manager, therefore agrees with the brewery who own the premises that he will apply for a protection order and then for the licence to be transferred into his name.

A *protection order* will allow Barnaby to sell intoxicating liquor of all descriptions pending the transfer of the justices' licence to him. This means that although he does not hold a justices' licence, the protection order will *protect* him from being prosecuted for selling intoxicating liquor until the licence is transferred into his name.

A protection order can also be applied for where the licensee is declared bankrupt which automatically disqualifies him from holding a justices' licence.

Barnaby telephones the local magistrates' court to check on procedure. He learns that he can apply for a protection order at any magistrates' session and that he does not need to wait until the next transfer sessions. He fills out an application form, inserting the date of the next magistrates' sessions which is 30 September. He sends the original application to the court together with a cheque made payable to The Clerk to the Justices for £4.00. He sends a copy to

# THE LICENSING HANDBOOK

the chief officer of Police and keeps a copy for himself. Barnaby notes that these copy applications need to be sent out at least seven days before the hearing date which does not include the day they are posted, the day they are received or the date of the hearing. He sends the letters by recorded delivery and completes a *certificate of service* to record what he has done (see *Form 4* on page 112).

Several days later Barnaby receives a telephone call from the constable at the local Police station who deals with licensing matters. He checks whether Barnaby has ever held a licence before and as he has not, asks him to supply him with two character references from professional people. He then asks him about his job and whether he has any criminal convictions pending or in the past. Barnaby is a little concerned about his drink driving conviction from seven years ago but the constable says he does not see this as a problem. Finally the constable asks him for his date of birth so that he can run standard computer checks on him.

The next day the constable telephones Barnaby to confirm that the Police have no objections to make about the protection order application. Barnaby is feeling a little nervous about going to court so the brewery agree to engage a solicitor for him. This is not strictly necessary but Barnaby feels more confident about it than having to do all the talking himself.

## The Hearing

The application is to take place on the following Thursday morning and Barnaby goes along to the local magistrates' court and has a brief discussion with his solicitor beforehand. He is asked to fill out a standard form for the justices giving details of name, occupation and licensing experience. He also gives the solicitor the certificate of service to hand into the justices clerk.

When the court starts the clerk announces the first application of the morning - a protection order for Moonrakers Wine Bar. The solicitor goes to the front of the court and gives brief details about the background to the application. Barnaby, standing at the witness stand, is then asked to take the oath. His solicitor asks him to

# 4. PROTECTION ORDERS AND TRANSFERS

confirm his name, address, occupation and whether he has any experience of licensing and familiarity with the licensing laws. He asks him if he knows of any reason why he should not hold a justices' licence and Barnaby replies that he does not. He is asked to confirm that he will be applying for the justices' licence for Moonrakers to be transferred into his name. He confirms that this is indeed the case.

The clerk to the justices states that no objections have been received from the Police and the magistrates declare the protection order granted.

Barnaby receives this in the post about ten days later. He can however serve alcohol before it physically arrives. He will now go ahead and apply for the licence to be transferred into his name.

## Transferring a Licence from One Person to Another

A licence transfer can only be applied for at the transfer sessions usually held once a month for the licensing district in question. It is worth noting that transfers can only be granted at the discretion of the justices and will only be granted where the holder of the existing licence has died, where incapability or illness prevents the current licensee from continuing as a licensee, where the licence holder is adjudicated bankrupt or enters into a voluntary arrangement, where the licence holder has given up or is about to give up occupation of the premises to the new occupier. Where an outgoing licensee has allowed the licence to lapse or failed to renew application can also be made for it to be transferred to the new occupier. If, for any reason, the justices refuse to transfer the licence, there is a right of appeal to the Crown Court.

Barnaby telephones the court and is told that the next transfer sessions are to be held on 1 November.

He completes the application form requesting a transfer (see *Form 5* on page 112) and takes a copy for himself and four others. He sends the original with a cheque for £12.50 made out to The Clerk to the Justices to the licensing justices' clerk at the magistrates' court and a copy to each of the following:

- The chief officer of Police;
- The local authority;
- The town council;
- Harry Moonshine, the outgoing licensee.

It is always worth telephoning the licensing justices clerk to check on the parties who must be given notice of the application as requirements can vary from area to area, especially in the London boroughs. A brief letter should be sent out with each application form explaining that a protection order was granted on 30 September and that Barnaby is now applying for the licence for Moonrakers Wine Bar to be transferred into his sole name. Each addressee (apart from the court) should be asked to confirm receipt of the application in writing and whether they have any objections to the transfer taking place.

All parties must be given twenty-one days' notice (which does not include the day of posting, the day of receipt or the day of the hearing). Barnaby sends the letters by registered post and again completes a certificate of service to confirm that he has served all relevant parties with the required notice.

There is no duty to display notice of the application at the premises or to advertise it in a local newspaper where a transfer is being sought.

Although Barnaby is allowed by the grant of the protection order to sell intoxicating liquor of all descriptions, the protection order will cease in its effect if the licence is not transferred to him by the end of the second transfer sessions following the grant of the protection order.

Over the next few weeks Barnaby receives letters from the Local Authority, the Town Council, Harry Moonshine and the Police confirming that they have received notice of his intention to transfer the justices' licence and that they have no objection to such a transfer taking place. He also receives a letter of confirmation from the licensing justices which states that his application will be heard at 2pm on 1 November.

# 4. PROTECTION ORDERS AND TRANSFERS

## The Hearing

On the afternoon of the application Barnaby again meets his solicitor in the area outside the Court room and hands him the certificate of service to give to the clerk to the justices. At 2pm everyone present enters the court room and takes their seats at the back. The clerk to the justices then reads out the name of the first application and its nature - Moonrakers Wine Bar, transfer of justices' licence.

Barnaby's solicitor goes to the front of the court and Barnaby waits with the usher by the witness stand. Barnaby's solicitor then gives a brief background to the matter and Barnaby is asked to swear an oath. The solicitor asks him to confirm his name and address and the justices then question him about his experience in the licensing trade and how long he has been a manager of Moonrakers Wine Bar. They also ask him if he has any formal training. Barnaby says he hasn't and the justices tell him that persons entrusted to hold justices' licences have a special duty to uphold and that they particularly like to see such persons holding a recognised certificate of training. They state that upon Barnaby giving an undertaking that he will undergo a recognised form of training they will agree to transfer the licence to him. Barnaby gives the undertaking and the licence is granted. The justices finally say that they remind all applicants of the laws regarding under age drinking as in their particular district it is something they are keen to eliminate. Barnaby says that he is well aware of the law in relation to this and upholds it at all times.

Two days later Barnaby receives a letter asking him to send the existing licence to the justices. As Harry has left it for this purpose he does so. It is usually advisable to take a licence to court and hand it in to the justices' clerk.

## Transferring a Justices' Licence from One Set of Premises to Another

The type of transfer where a licence is transferred from one set of premises to another, as opposed to from one person to another, is known as a *removal*. There are two types of removals - *ordinary* and *special*.

## Ordinary and Special Removals

Ordinary removals are where a licence is transferred from one set of premises to another for any reason other than those for which a special removal is granted. Special removals are granted where the premises to which the licence relates have been rendered unfit for business by reason of fire, tempest or other unforeseeable disaster or where the premises have been or are about to be pulled down or occupied under the provisions of any Act of Parliament for the improvement of public highways or any other business.

An ordinary removal can be granted to any set of premises within the licensing district, whether or not the licence is being removed from a set of premises in the same district or a different district. A special removal, however can only be granted where both sets of premises are within the same licensing district. Where a licence is to be removed to premises outside the licensing area, the application must be made to the licensing justices in the new area.

Special removals are only granted to premises licensed under "old" on licences. An old on licence is one which was in force on 15 August 1904 for the sale of intoxicating liquor for consumption on the premises other than wine alone.

A removal (whether ordinary or special) will only be granted where no objection to it being removed is received from the owner of the premises from which it is to be removed or from the licence holder, where the licence in question is an on licence. Where it is an off licence, it will be granted where no objections are received from either the licence holder or any other persons other than him or the owner of the premises whom the justices consider have a right to object to the removal taking place.

# 4. PROTECTION ORDERS AND TRANSFERS

## Applying for Removals

An application for an ordinary or special removal is made in the same way as an application for a new justices' licence. Notice of the application is given to the same parties (including the fire authority for the area) and also to the owner of the premises. In the case of an ordinary removal of both an on or off licence, a plan of the premises where the licence is to be removed must accompany the application sent to the clerk to the justices and full details given of the premises from which the licence is to be removed. An application for either type of removal must state the premises from which it is sought to remove the licence. Notice of the application must be displayed on or near the premises and advertised in the local press.

# 5. VARYING LICENCES

## Applications for Variations

An application to vary the type of liquor that can be sold under an existing licence may be made at any licensing sessions. This can be done when the licence is renewed or transferred but the justices will only permit such a variation where the premises' owner consents. Such variations can though only be applied for by holders of licences which were in force on or before 3 August 1961 and regularly renewed after that date. Anyone else must apply for a new licence.

Where the premises are in a New Town, the justices have a power to delay granting any variation until they receive confirmation from the Town Committee that does not object to the variation.

Conditions can be attached to any variations that are made and may be in addition to, or instead of, any conditions which already attach to the licence.

## Variations to Permitted Licensing Hours

Application to vary the permitted licensing hours is made by applying for an *order of exemption*. The application can be made by the holder of an on licence or by the secretary of a registered club. If successful, the order will allow the sale of intoxicating liquor outside the normal licensing hours but within a specified time period. There are two types of orders of exemption - general and special and they are more commonly referred to as "*extensions*".

## General Orders of Exemption

General orders of exemption would be appropriate where a licence holder wishes licensing hours to be permanently extended for the benefit of a particular group of people.

# 5. VARYING LICENCES

Such an extension would be appropriate where, for example, there is a need established by a particular group of persons such as all-night workers at a market.

## Special Orders of Exemption

Special orders of exemption would be appropriate in circumstances where hours are to be extended for a one off occasion such as a ball or dinner where the bar is to stay open later than usual. The length of the extension granted will be determined by what the law considers reasonable. Application can be made by the holder of a justices' licence or by the secretary of a registered club.

## Supper Hours and Restaurant Certificates

Application can be made for a supper hours or restaurant certificate to allow licensed premises to sell intoxicating liquor in the gap between permitted licensing hours on Christmas Day and for an extra hour on each weekday evening after the end of the permitted licensing hours. The reason for the application must be to serve or supply persons eating table meals with drinks - that is, it must be ancillary to the consumption of a meal and in a part of the premises usually set apart for dining at a table.

Application can be made by the holder of a justices' licence or secretary of a registered club where the premises in question are able to accommodate the service of meals and where there is a habitual service of meals whether that service is actual or merely intended.

Before granting a supper hours or restaurant certificate, the justices must be satisfied that the premises are structurally suitable for providing meals and intend to provide "substantial refreshment" to persons who frequent them. They must also be satisfied that the supply of intoxicating liquor is ancillary to the consumption of meals eaten at tables in a designated area. "Substantial refreshment" means food actually consumed at a table provided for that purpose as opposed to take-aways or bar meals, but what actually constitutes a meal is a question for the justices to decide.

## Application for a Supper Hours or Restaurant Certificate

The applicant must serve a copy of his application to apply for a supper hours or restaurant certificate on the clerk to the licensing justices and the chief officer of Police at least seven days in advance of the date of the intended hearing. The application (see *Form 6* on page 114) can also state the date on which it is intended for the certificate to come into effect which must be no less than fourteen days later than the date of the application. If this is not included in the application then a separate notice must be served on the chief officer of Police fourteen clear days in advance of the intended commencement date giving details of that commencement date.

A supper hours/restaurant certificate remains in force until it is withdrawn. Notice may be served on the holder, however if any question of withdrawal is raised, no less than seven days in advance of the annual licensing sessions. When the justices convene, they will then consider whether or not the certificate is to be withdrawn.

Likewise, if the holder of the certificate wishes its operation to cease, notice must be given to the chief officer of Police no less than fourteen days in advance of 4 April. It will then expire on that date.

## Special Hours Certificates

Special hours certificates extend the permitted licensing hours for premises which serve meals and provide entertainment in the form of music and dancing. Hours are generally extended until 2am provided that music and dancing continue until that time. Drinking up time is thirty minutes and both registered clubs and the holders of justices' licences may apply.

In the case of licensed premises, the justices must be satisfied that the premises hold a current licence for music and dancing and that

# 5. VARYING LICENCES

all of or part of the premises are structurally capable of accommodating persons for music and dancing and substantial refreshment to which the sale and supply of intoxicating liquor is ancillary.

For licensed premises, application is made to licensing justices and if they are satisfied that the above conditions are complied with, they have a general discretion as to whether or not to grant the certificate. It may be granted with or without limitations such as restricting the operation of the certificate to the days of the week when music, dancing and refreshment are provided on the premises or to times of the day or periods of the year. It may also state a time at which the dancing is to start. The justices are not under any duty to attach such limitations but simply have a power to do so if they consider it prudent. Limitations cannot restrict the life of the certificate, only its effect and it will be effective from the commencement date notified to the chief officer of Police. Any limitations attached can be varied by the licence holder making a further application to the licensing justices.

Once granted, a special hours certificate remains in force until it is revoked. In some circumstances the Police may apply for it to be revoked on the grounds of disorderly conduct taking place on the premises.

## Application for a Special Hours Certificate

For premises which are licensed, notice in writing of an intention to apply for a special hours certificate must be given to the chief officer of Police at least twenty-one days in advance of applying to the justices for the certificate to be granted. Such notice must contain the address of the licensed premises, be signed by the applicant or his agent and contain the intended commencement date (see *Form 7* on page 115).

A notice giving details of the application must be displayed at or near the premises in question for a period of no less than seven days. Notice must also be advertised in the local paper. Both of these notices must be displayed no less than fourteen and no more than twenty-eight days in advance of the application being made to the justices.

Any person who wishes to oppose the granting of the special hours certificate or who wishes limitations or variations to be attached to it, must give notice in writing to the applicant and the clerk to the justices no later than seven days in advance of the licensing sessions at which the application is to be heard. Such a notice must contain the general terms in which the opposition is being made. Any failure to observe these rules with regard to time periods will result in the justices being unable to entertain the objection.

A right of appeal exists where the justices refuse to grant a special hours certificate, revoke or fail to revoke it or attach or fail to attach conditions to it when granted. It should be noted that only a chief officer of Police has the right to appeal against a failure to revoke a certificate or a failure to attach limitations to it and in the latter case, may only do so in any event where the Police have previously appeared before the justices and made representations for limitations to be attached.

It is possible for a supper hours certificate and a special hours certificate to run concurrently for the same set of premises.

## Extended Hours Orders

Extended hours orders extend permitted licensing hours for premises which provide live entertainment. Live entertainment means where persons are actually present and performing at the premises and does not extend to any other form of entertainment.

Extended hours orders can only be applied for by premises which possess a supper hours/restaurant certificate and which are suitably structurally adapted for the purpose of providing live entertainment and used or intended to be used for habitually providing musical or live entertainment together with substantial refreshment. The supply of intoxicating liquor must once again be ancillary to the supply of the substantial refreshment and entertainment.

If granted, the extended hours order will extend licensing hours to 1am on week days on which the live entertainment takes place and

# 5. VARYING LICENCES

where the extra time is for the sale supply and consumption of liquor whilst the entertainment is taking place. Drinking up time is 30 minutes. Both licensed premises and registered clubs can apply for an extended hours order.

Application is made in the same way as and served on the same parties as those for an application for a new justices' licence. Where such an order is granted the holder of the justices' licence for the premises in question must, within fourteen days, give notice of the extended hours order to the chief officer of Police and send him a copy. Failure to do so can result in a fine.

The extended hours order will cease in its effect when the on licence lapses but will remain in force where a licence is renewed by way of a transfer or renewal. The order will be revoked however where the justices or magistrates consider that the premises are not being used for the stated purpose, for example, where there is no provision of substantial refreshment or live entertainment but merely an extension of drinking hours. Similarly, revocation can occur where the conduct of persons using the premises is considered undesirable or where persons living nearby are affected by it.

The order may be limited in its operation to part of the premises, particular days of the week, days of the year or to an earlier time than 1am if it appears reasonable to do so, having regard to all the circumstances of the matter including the comfort and convenience of the occupants of neighbouring premises.

The order comes into force as soon as it is granted.

## Restrictions on Permitted Licensing Hours

In the same way that variations and extensions can be made to permitted licensing hours, restrictions can also apply. Restrictions cannot, however be applied to off licences or occasional licences. A restriction order may prevent the sale of liquor at any time between 2.30pm and 5.30pm on weekdays other than Good Friday and between 3pm and 7pm on Sundays and Good Friday.

A restriction order can only be applied for by a chief officer of Police, by a person living or carrying on business in the neighbourhood or by someone on his behalf, of by a person in charge of an educational establishment in the area.

A restriction order can be made on the grounds that it is desirable to avoid or reduce disturbance or annoyance to persons living or working in the neighbourhood, to reduce disorderly conduct at the premises or within their immediate vicinity or by persons using the premises, to customers of businesses in the neighbourhood or to persons attending, or in charge of those attending, educational establishments in the neighbourhood.

A restriction order can be granted for a maximum period of twelve months and will expire after its term ceases. The licence holder can appeal against it but must wait until six months have elapsed before doing so.

## Seasonal and Early Closing Licences

Any person applying for a justices on licence may also request that there are no permitted hours at certain times of the year. This would be appropriate, for example, at a seaside hotel. A condition is attached to the on licence which makes it a seasonal licence. Such an application can be made at any licensing sessions or upon an application for a renewal, transfer or removal. Similarly, application can be made for an early closing licence.

## Displaying Notices

Under s89 of the Licensing Act 1964 where licensing hours have been modified by a general order of exemption, extended in restaurants including those whose hours have been extended to provide entertainment or where a special hours certificate has been granted, the licence holder must post a notice in a conspicuous place stating the effect of the order or provision and if it is to apply on certain days only, to make this clear. If this section is not adhered to the person responsible will be liable to a fine.

# 6. OCCASIONAL LICENCES AND PERMISSIONS

## Occasional Licences

An occasional licence authorises the holder of a justices' on licence to sell intoxicating liquor at some place other than the premises to which his licence relates, for example at a race meeting or outdoor musical event. It is not granted by the licensing justices but by the petty sessional division for the locality.

Application is made to the court for the area in which the proposed function is to be held and may therefore be a different court from that which deals with the more usual applications to vary the terms of a licence.

Application is made by completing a standard form (see *Form 8* on page 116) and should detail the date and time of the function, the hours on which it is to take place, the time it is to finish and the nature and venue of the event.

Where the proposed function is one calendar month or more after the application is received by the court, the application can be dealt with entirely by post which means that no appearance at court is necessary. For a postal application, three copies of the application must be sent to the relevant court together with a cheque for £4 made payable to The Clerk to the Justices. The result of the application will be sent out by post at a later date together with the licence if the application is successful.

If the function is to take place less than one calendar month from the date on which the court receives the application, it will be necessary to attend a court hearing. Two copies of the application together with a cheque for £4 made payable as before must be sent to the court.

In both instances a copy of the application should be sent to the chief officer of Police for the area in which the function is to take place.

An occasional licence cannot be granted for a period exceeding three consecutive weeks nor be granted for functions taking place on Christmas Day or Good Friday.

## Occasional Permissions

Occasional permissions are relevant to small organisations only to allow them to sell intoxicating liquor at functions connected with their business operations for a period not in excess of twenty-four hours. Permissions are granted to individual officers of organisations considered eligible for such a grant which then allow the organisation or branch to sell intoxicating liquor during a specified time period.

Applications for occasional permissions are heard at the licensing sessions for the relevant district and two copies must be served on the clerk to the licensing justices no less than one month in advance of the date of the intended function. The clerk will then send one copy to the chief officer of Police although in some areas it is the responsibility of the applicant to serve this notice. It is always advisable to telephone the local licensing justices department as procedure can vary from district to district. The justices clerk will then notify the applicant of the date and time the application is to be heard. This type of application is only relevant to small organisations and not to licensed premises or clubs.

## Application for an Occasional Permission

The application must contain:

- The name and address of the applicant;
- The name of the organisation intending to hold the function;
- The reason for the organisation being in existence;
- The name of the branch of the organisation which intends to hold the function;
- The applicant's position within the organisation or branch of the organisation;

# 6. OCCASIONAL LICENCES AND PERMISSIONS

- The date, nature and venue of the proposed function;
- The hours of the function;
- The type of intoxicating liquor intended to be sold at it;
- Details of any occasional permissions granted during the previous twelve months to the organisation or branch of the organisation.

# 7. RENEWING A JUSTICES' LICENCE

## The Need to Renew a Licence

Once granted, a justices' licence does not run indefinitely but must be renewed at certain periods. Licensing periods mean a period of three years beginning with 5 April 1989 and are composed of subsequent three year periods. Licences need to be renewed at the expiry of the licensing period currently in effect. So a licence itself does not run for three years from the date it is granted but only until the date the licensing period in which it is granted is due to expire. This will be shown on the licence itself. If a licence is granted within the last three months of a licensing period it will not need to be renewed until the end of the next licensing period.

A licence may also be renewed when an application is made to transfer or remove it.

Applications for the renewal of a justices' licence must be made to the annual brewster sessions held in the first fortnight of February and not at the transfer sessions held during the rest of the year. The only time a licence can be renewed at a transfer session is where the justices are satisfied with the reason for not having renewed a licence at the appropriate Brewster sessions. Application must be made to the Brewster sessions due to be held before the expiry of the licensing period. Where a licence expires because it has not been renewed, an application for a new licence will be treated as an application for a renewal where it is made before the next Brewster sessions take place and where the justices are satisfied with the reasons for it not having previously been renewed.

Application for renewal is made to the Clerk to the Justices and the applicant will only be required to attend in person at the Brewster sessions where objections to the renewal of the licence are received. Otherwise the renewal will be dealt with by post. The justices may themselves object to the renewal where they are dissatisfied with the way the premises have been run or with the conduct at them.

# 7. RENEWING A JUSTICES' LICENCE

The justices have a discretion as to whether or not to renew a licence but the extent of that discretion depends upon the type of licence being renewed. For example, in the case of "old on licences" or "old beerhouse licences" they can only refuse to renew the licence where certain criteria are not met. Old on licences are those licences in force on 15 August 1904 for the sale of intoxicating liquor other than wine alone. Old beerhouse licences are licences for the sale of beer or cider with or without wine which were granted and in force on 15 August 1904 in respect of premises for which a licence was in force on 1 May 1869.

If the renewal is refused however, there is a right of appeal to the Crown Court and the licence will remain in force until the appeal has been heard. Most ordinary on and off licences are renewed without any problem and without the applicant needing to attend court.

A licence can also come to an end by what is known as *forfeiture* which occurs when certain events prescribed by the law occur which automatically terminate the licence. The court can also make an order under which the licence will be forfeited.

## Forfeiture and Revocation

Automatic forfeiture will occur where, for example, the licence holder is convicted of allowing his premises to be used as a brothel or where he is convicted on a second offence for selling or exposing for sale, any intoxicating liquor of whatever description without a licence or at premises where he is not permitted to sell it.

Forfeiture by order of the court will occur where, for example, a licensee is convicted for a second or subsequent time of selling or permitting the sale of alcoholic liquor to persons under eighteen years of age. He will also be responsible for the actions of his staff if they sell alcohol to persons under age even if he is not physically there when it happens.

Licences can also be revoked. This usually follows an application by the Police following allegations of disorderly conduct or complaints by neighbours living in the vicinity of the licensed premises who are being affected by noise and disturbance. An application to revoke a licence can be made by any person or by the licensing justices themselves but must be notified to the holder of the licence and the clerk to the justices at least twenty-one days in advance of the licensing sessions at which the application to revoke is to be heard excluding the Brewster Sessions at which renewal of the licence is to be heard. An application to revoke a licence must contain the general grounds for doing so and if a licence is revoked, there is a right of appeal. The licence will however remain in force until the appeal has been heard or until the time for making an appeal has expired.

## Surrendering a Justices' Licence

A licence can be surrendered by the licensee where he wishes the conditions attached to it to be varied. In such circumstances he can make an application for a new licence detailing the variations required. These will then be granted upon the surrender of the existing licence. A licence may also be surrendered where a licensee wishes a new licence for different premises to come into effect upon the expiry of the current licence. The provisions for surrendering a licence are not expressly provided for within the law but have become accepted as tenable practice.

## Licences in Suspense

Where licensed premises are or are about to be the subject of a compulsory purchase order, a licence may be suspended provided that the Commissioners of Customs & Excise are satisfied that the operation of the business is to be temporarily suspended.

Where an application is made to suspend a licence, a certificate will be granted detailing the suspension. During the suspension the licence can be transferred or removed but otherwise does not have an active life.

If a suspended licence is removed to other premises it becomes active again. An application must be made beforehand to the

## 7. RENEWING A JUSTICES' LICENCE

licensing justices for the relevant area to gain their approval that the licensee is a fit and proper person to hold a justices' licence. Once this approval is forthcoming the licensee serves notice on the clerk to the justices of his intention to resume the business and the licence will be restored from the time of giving that notice.

Licences may also be suspended where a business has been operating from temporary premises and removing the licence to other premises is impractical. Licences in suspense can be extinguished when the justices feel suspension is no longer justified.

# 8. RESTAURANT LICENSING

## Part IV Licences

Restaurant licences are commonly referred to as *Part IV licences* and take their name from Part IV of the Licensing Act 1964 which gives them their authority. Restaurant licences allow alcoholic beverages to be served with meals and there are three types:

- The restaurant licence;
- The residential license;
- The combined restaurant and residential licence.

The restaurant licence is granted to premises to permit the sale and supply of alcohol which is ancillary to a meal although there is no requirement that alcohol must be served with the meal. Alcohol can only be supplied to persons eating at the premises and where the premises themselves are of the type which habitually serve or intend to serve lunch or dinner or a combination of both.

The residential licence is granted to premises used or intended to be used on a regular basis to provide board and lodging. Liquor cannot be sold or supplied to anyone who is not staying there but can be sold or supplied to the friends of those who are staying there. This includes supplying alcohol for consumption off the premises, for example, with a packed lunch.

The combined restaurant and residential licence is granted to premises which qualify for both a restaurant and residential licence and liquor can only be sold or supplied in the same way as it would for individual restaurant or residential licences.

An implied condition of the grant of any of the above licences is that suitable beverages other than intoxicating liquor will be equally available.

Where the justices grant a new residential licence or combined restaurant and residential licence, they must, unless there are

# 8. RESTAURANT LICENSING

exceptional circumstances, attach a condition to the licence that a room will be provided for persons using the premises for board and lodging for the provision of meals and drinks. This room must not be a room used for sleeping accommodation.

## Applications for Restaurant and Similar Licences

All three licences can be applied for at both Brewster and transfer sessions and the justices' power to refuse to grant such licences is much narrower than it is for justices' licences. An application should be made in the same format as for a full justices' on licence, indicating on the form that it is the applicant's intention to apply to the magistrates to insert in the justices' licence granted such conditions as are required for it to be granted as a restaurant licence.

An ordinary on licence can be turned into a Part IV licence when a party makes an application for it to be renewed, transferred or removed. The consent of the owner of the premises must be obtained beforehand and conditions will be attached to the licence which will convert it into a Part IV licence.

Where a licence is required for both the sale of liquor to the public and for consumption by diners with their meal, a full justices' on licence should be sought. This would be the case where, for example, an Indian restaurant wished to serve customers waiting for takeaways meals with alcoholic drinks from the bar in addition to serving alcoholic drinks to diners eating on the premises. If a restaurant has a bar purely to serve those eating on premises with drinks, then a restaurant licence would be the appropriate application to make.

## Disqualifications and Prohibitions

A person convicted of certain offences while he is in possession of a Part IV licence may be disqualified from holding the licence or the premises to which it relates prohibited from being licensed. Such a disqualification may either disqualify a person from holding or obtaining specified types of licence for a stated period or prevent a licence from being granted to anyone for the premises at which the offence was committed or a combination of both. Offences which can result in such disqualification or prohibition include selling liquor in breach of the licensing laws or allowing gambling on the premises. There is a right of appeal and the justices have a discretion to suspend the operation of the disqualification or prohibition until the appeal has been heard.

Any person affected by the disqualification or prohibition can, while it is in force, apply to the magistrates' court for it to be revoked or varied by reducing the period of disqualification specified in the order. A subsequent right of appeal to the Crown Court is available. Any such application to revoke or vary a disqualification or prohibition must be served on the chief officer of Police for the area at the time of making the application.

## Displaying a Notice

The holder of a Part IV licence must display a notice on the premises stating his name and sufficient words to convey the fact that he is licensed to sell liquor for consumption on the premises with meals. This notice must contain the word "licensed" but no separate notice need be displayed stating that he is licensed to sell liquor.

## Case Histories:

Mohammed and Sujata Khan have recently taken over premises which they intend to run as an Indian restaurant. The restaurant is to cater for seated diners as well as provide a takeaway menu. Additionally they want to be able to serve alcohol to diners with their meals and provide it to people waiting in the bar area for their takeaways.

They apply for a justices' licence to allow them to serve alcohol to people who are not eating meals at the restaurant and also to people who are.

# 8. RESTAURANT LICENSING

Giovanni and Jenna are the managers of an Italian restaurant. Drinks are only available to persons eating meals on the premises. They apply for a restaurant licence rather than a justices' licence.

# 9. CLUBS

## Introduction

Alcohol may be sold in clubs either under the authority of a registration certificate granted under the Licensing Act 1964 or by the authority given by a justices' licence. A registration certificate can only be refused on certain specified grounds whereas a justices' licence can be refused for a much wider range of reasons.

A licence granted to a club will usually have several conditions attached to it such as a condition which prohibits sales of alcohol to non-members of the club and that a period of forty-eight hours must elapse between a person being nominated for membership and being admitted as a member.

## Registration Certificates: Prerequisites

Application for a registration certificate is made to the magistrates' court and one certificate may cover any number of premises which are used by the same club. Once granted, the certificate will remain in force for a period of twelve months. After that time it may be renewed and a second or subsequent renewal can be extended for up to ten years. Application for renewal must be made no less than twenty-eight days before the certificate is due to expire.

Before a club can apply for a registration certificate its membership rules must fulfil the following conditions:

- two days must elapse between nomination or application for membership and actually being given that membership and the same time period also applies to those who are not nominated or who do not make a formal application;
- the club must be established and conducted in good faith as a club with a membership that exceeds twenty-five persons;

# 9. CLUBS

- intoxicating liquor must not be or intended to be supplied to members at the club premises other than by or on behalf of the club;
- the purchase and supply of intoxicating liquor by the club is carried out by an elective committee, that is, by members elected to the club's committee for a term exceeding one year but no more than five years;
- no person must receive a commission, percentage etc. of sales from the purchase of alcohol at the club's expense;
- no person must derive any monetary benefit from selling the alcohol at the club apart from the monetary benefit to the club as a whole.

If the above criteria are satisfied, a club may then apply to the magistrates for a certificate authorising it to sell intoxicating liquor at the club's premises.

## Application for a Registration Certificate

An application for a registration certificate must:

- state the name, objectives and address of the club and state that a list of members' names and addresses is kept at the club;
- confirm that the club meets the requirements necessary to be granted a certificate;
- have a document attached to it specifying the names and addresses of the persons who manage the club's affairs and those of any other committee, if relevant, who are responsible for purchasing and supplying intoxicating liquor for the club;
- set out the rules of the club or set these out in a document attached to the application. In the case of an application for a renewal of the certificate, these should detail any changes which have been made to the club rules since the certificate was granted or since it was last renewed. If no changes have been made this must be specifically stated;

- provide details about the club premises together with a statement to the effect that they are habitually occupied and used for club purposes;
- state the times at which the club is or is proposed to be open to its members and the hours fixed by the rules of the club (if appropriate);
- specify the interest the club holds in the premises - whether they are leasehold, freehold or held in trust and the name and address of the person to whom rent is paid, if relevant;
- provide details of any other premises used for club purposes and the name and address of the person to whom rent is paid, if relevant;
- state details of any liabilities the club may have (including future liabilities) such as the terms of any loans or details of any charges attaching to the premises and the name and address of the person who has made the loan or registered the charge. If there are no liabilities this must be clearly stated. In the case of an application for a renewal of the certificate, details of any indebtedness incurred since the grant of the certificate or last renewal must be stated;
- give details of any other premises not detailed above - for example premises which have been used by the club during the last twelve months but which are no longer being used. Details of any interest held in such premises must be given together with the name and address of the person to whom rent was paid if relevant. If no such premises have been used this must be clearly stated;
- contain the name and address of any third party who may have paid the rent under the lease (if appropriate) on any of the premises currently in use or used within the last twelve months by the club.

## Objections

The magistrates can only refuse to grant or renew a certificate where properly made objections are forwarded and, in the case of a refusal, they must put their reasons for doing so in writing.

# 9. CLUBS

Some examples of where they might refuse to renew or grant a certificate are where they consider that a person who is likely to take an active part in the management of the club is unfit to do so. A certificate cannot be granted for premises which have been disqualified from holding a justices' licence or where, within the last twelve months, those premises have been subject to forfeiture or there has been a refusal to renew a licence because of it being revoked. If the club uses other premises authorised to supply intoxicating liquor by a justices' licence they may refuse to issue or renew a certificate where they consider that to do so may result in the abuse of the licensing laws.

Objections to a certificate being granted or renewed can only be made by the chief officer of Police, the local council or any person who is affected by way of his interest in or occupation of other premises. Objections can only be made on certain specified grounds:

- that the application does not give the information required by law or is incomplete or inaccurate;
- that the premises are not suitable for their proposed purpose because of their condition and character when considered in proportion to the size and nature of the club;
- that the club does not satisfy the conditions for making an application for a registration certificate;
- that the club is conducted in a disorderly manner or for an unlawful purpose and where the rules governing the election and admission of new members are repeatedly broken;
- that the club premises, including those which are not registered, are habitually used for an unlawful purpose or where illegal sales of alcohol have taken place within the last twelve months and/or have been supplied to persons who are not supposed to be supplied with it, such as persons other than members or their guests, or that the club is frequented by criminals and prostitutes on a regular basis.

If the objection made relates to one part of the premises only, or to one set of premises where the club is active, the court may refuse to issue a certificate or may only renew it for part of the premises or in respect of a particular building.

Where the objection is made under one of the first three grounds, the court must refuse the application if it is satisfied with the circumstances put before it although it may abstain from refusing to renew or grant the certificate where steps can be taken to remove the source of the objection.

Where a club is registered in respect of any premises and the court refuses to grant or renew a certificate on the last three grounds, the court may order that the premises are to remain unoccupied by any club for a specified period which must not exceed one year unless the premises have been the subject of a previous order on similar terms. In such circumstances an order will not usually exceed five years.

## Procedure

Application for a registration certificate is made to the magistrates' court with jurisdiction for the area in which the club premises are situated and is heard by not less than two magistrates.

The application is made by lodging the application form and two copies with the magistrates' clerk. He will then send a copy of it to the local council and the chief officer of Police for the area. This is also the procedure to follow where the application is for the renewal or variation of a certificate. In all instances, the application must be signed by the chairman or secretary of the club.

Where the fire authority for the area is a separate body from the local authority, the magistrates' clerk will also send it a copy of the application. The fire authority has a right of inspection and objection if they consider the premises unsuitable for the club's intended purpose bearing in mind the size, condition and character of the premises in relation to the nature and membership of the club.

Notice of the application must be displayed at or near the premises in question identifying the name and address of the club where it can be read by the public for a period of seven days starting from the date of making the application or advertised in a newspaper

# 9. CLUBS

circulating in the area where the premises are situated. Where application is being made for the renewal of a certificate for different, enlarged or additional premises, this procedure must also be followed but not for an ordinary renewal or variation such as an application for a restaurant/supper hours certificate or for a special hours certificate.

Any person wishing to object to the application must do so within twenty-eight days of the application being lodged with the magistrates' court and must clearly state the grounds on which the objections are being made. Objections must be sent to the court who will send a copy to the applicant.

In the case of applications for renewal or variation of a certificate, the court may deal with the matter without the club attending to make any representations. If however the application is refused or the requested period for a renewal is shortened, a representative from the club will be required to attend. The club may be represented by a member of its committee or an authorised officer.

## Registration Certificates in General

Where a new club is applying for registration the magistrates will assume that the club satisfies the conditions required for registration where the rules of the club conform with Schedule 7 of the Licensing Act 1964. These include:

- that the club is managed by one or more elective committees one of which is concerned with the general management of its affairs;
- the committee must be capable of convening a general meeting at any time with reasonable notice;
- that annual general meetings are held without a gap of more than fifteen months between them;
- that voting at general meetings is confined to members and all those entitled to use the club premises have an entitlement to vote, such persons must have equal voting rights unless the club rules allow differently, for example, only allowing voting by persons above a certain age;

- Any changes to the club rules must be notified within twenty-eight days of their alteration to the chief officer of Police and the clerk to the local authority. Failure to do so may result in the secretary being fined.

Registered clubs are an exception to the general rule that a justices' licence is required before intoxicating liquor can be sold, but to prevent any abuse of the registration process, the court may attach certain conditions to the certificate which restrict or over rule changes made to the rules of the club which might permit sales of alcohol where these have not been authorised by the court. Therefore if a club were granted registered status and it then changed its rules to allow alcohol to be supplied in other premises it owned or occupied, which were not registered, the court could impose conditions to over rule the club rules in order to prevent abuse of the licensing laws.

Where the rules of the club are altered so as to allow premises to sell liquor which were not authorised for such sales at the time of applying for registration, or at the last application for renewal, the alteration to the rules will not dispose of the need to obtain a justices' licence until the club secretary has given the requisite notice of the alteration to the rules to the chief officer of Police and the clerk to the local authority within twenty-eight days of the alteration being made.

Conditions can only be imposed, varied or revoked when the club makes an application for renewal of the certificate or where a complaint is made against the club by the local authority or chief officer of Police.

The clerk to the justices keeps a register of those clubs which hold registration certificates, which also details the opening hours applicable to them as fixed by the rules of the club. The Police and local authority have a right to inspect club premises on giving forty-eight hours' notice upon receipt of an application for a certificate. Any inspection must take place within the fourteen days following the application being made. The club must be open for inspection at reasonable times if so requested by statutory bodies and will be given

# 9. CLUBS

a fee for such an inspection taking place unless the inspection is by the Police, local authority or Customs & Excise officers.

Any changes to the club which might affect the register must be given in writing to the clerk to the justices within forty-two days of the changes being made and if not, both the chairman and the secretary may be liable to a fine.

A club has the right of appeal to the Crown Court from a magistrates' court's refusal to issue or renew a certificate where it prohibits the use and occupation of the premises for club purposes or against conditions imposed on the certificate or where the certificate is cancelled.

Clubs which do not qualify for registration status or which do not wish to become registered can apply for a justices' licence to allow the club to supply members and their guests with alcohol. A justices' licence can be applied for whether or not other premises owned or occupied by the club carry a registration certificate.

Where a club is registered, it cannot supply liquor other than at the registered premises. Where it is licensed this ruling does not apply.

A justices' licence must be granted in the name of an officer of the club nominated to hold such a licence by the club and the usual rights and obligations of a justices' licence attach to him personally.

Where a club is registered in respect of other premises it uses, and applies for a justices' licence for those premises, the justices must be satisfied that registration would not serve the purposes for which the justices' licence is being sought. They must also be satisfied that the grant of a licence will not give rise to abuse of the permitted licensing hours. A justices' licence may contain conditions forbidding or restricting the sale of liquor to non club members and in such cases the justices will insert a clause in the licence exempting the licence holder from statutory compliance with regard to notices being displayed at the premises.

## Permitted Hours

The permitted hours for a registered club are the same as those permitted by a justices' licence although a club can specify its own hours. These cannot however, be outside those permitted by law and are subject to the approval of the Magistrates at the time of applying for the registration certificate.

## Supper Hours and Restaurant Certificate

The secretary of a registered club may apply for a supper hours or restaurant certificate where there are suitable facilities for providing and serving meals and, in the opinion of the magistrates, the premises themselves are suitably adapted for such a purpose. Such an application is treated as a variation to the registration certificate and the procedure to follow is the same as for applying for a registration certificate.

## Special Hours Certificates

A registered club may wish to apply for a special hours certificate where, for example, a dinner dance is to take place. A special hours certificate is the appropriate extension for a club to apply for where meals are consumed on premises during an evening when music and dancing are also to take place. If a club sells or supplies intoxicating liquor, it will either do so under the authority of a justices' licences or registration certificate. Where it is authorised to sell intoxicating liquor under a justices' licence, application for a special hours certificate is made to the licensing justices for the area. The club must obtain a certificate from the body with authority for music and dancing in the area stating that the premises are considered suitably structurally adapted for music and dancing before any such application will be considered.

Where the club is authorised to sell intoxicating liquor under a registration certificate, application for a special hours certificate is made to the magistrates' court. Before any such application is made it must also obtain a certificate from the body with authority for

# 9. CLUBS

music and dancing in the area stating that the premises are suitably adapted for music and dancing (usually the local authority). There is no set procedure for applying for these certificates and enquiry should be made of the authority as to how the application should be presented. Once acquired, the certificate in both cases can be sent with the application for the special hours certificate and will take effect from the day the secretary or licensee of the club gives it in writing to the chief officer of Police. This should be done fourteen clear days in advance of the hearing date.

An application for a special hours certificate is treated as an application to vary a registration certificate and is made in the same way as such an application.

## Conditions on Special Hours Certificates

A special hours certificate may be granted with certain conditions attached to it and may, for example, only permit extended hours on certain days of the year or on certain days of the week. The certificate remains in force until revoked and does not require renewal. Its effect is to extend permitted licensing hours until 2am (3am in some areas of London) if music and dancing continue until that time. However the justices may set a commencement time as a condition of the certificate being granted.

## Extended Hours Orders

An extended hours order is the licensing extension to seek where premises provide live entertainment by performers actually at the premises. It can only be granted where the premises already hold a supper hours certificate and where the premises are considered suitable for providing such entertainment and refreshment and regularly do so or intend to do so. The sale and supply of liquor must be ancillary to this. The general effect of an extended hours order is to extend permitted licensing hours to 1am on weekdays on which the live entertainment is provided to allow intoxicating liquor to be supplied whilst the entertainment continues.

Again, the procedure is that stated in the application for a registration certificate. Application is made to the magistrates' court for the area and once granted, the chief officer of Police must be given written notice of it within fourteen days and sent a copy of the order. An extended hours order does not need renewing every year but will continue to be effective for the life of the licence to which it relates. The order comes into effect as soon as it is made but may be limited to certain parts of the premises or to specific weekdays and is always granted at the discretion of the magistrates. It can be revoked if subsequent disturbance or annoyance is caused to neighbouring premises.

## Extending Nightclubs' Hours

Nightclubs wishing to extend their hours must apply for a *section 77 licence* which permits the serving of alcohol outside of normal licensing hours. It is a condition for granting a section 77 licence that hot food must be served. A section 77 licence is also known as a special hours' certificate and if an application is made and the justices are satisfied that:

- a music and dancing licence is in force for the premises in question;
- all or part of the premises is structurally adapted and *bona fide* used or intended to be used for the purpose of providing for persons attending those premises with music, dancing and substantial refreshment to which the sale of intoxicating liquor is ancillary.

Once this is established the justices will grant the application. This may be with or without limitations which can restrict the intended activities to certain parts of the premises or certain days of the week.

"Licensed premises" in this context means premises for which a justices' licence is in force, and a "music and dancing licence" means

# 9. CLUBS

one granted by the licensing authority under the statutory regulations for music and dancing, that is, an entertainment licence.

Therefore a nightclub will need to obtain a section 77 licence from the magistrates' court and an entertainment licence from the council. The hours to which premises will be allowed to open to will depend on the magistrates for the area. In some parts of the country nightclubs can stay open no later than 2am. In others it can be as late as 6am. A section 77 licence must be renewed each year and an application form for both a new application and a renewal can be obtained from the local magistrates' court.

# 10. THE LICENSING OF MARRIAGE VENUES

## Approval of Venues for Civil Marriages

The Marriage Act 1994 allows public premises to be licensed for the purposes of carrying out civil marriage ceremonies.

A licence is granted to a set of premises by the county council (or London borough) with jurisdiction for the area in which the premises are situated. A fee is payable which is set by the council itself rather than by law. In Wiltshire, for example, the cost in February 1997 was £800.

## The Application for a Marriage Licence

Application is made for the approval of the premises as a venue for civil marriages using a standard form supplied by the council.

It is the proprietor of the premises who makes the application and, where it is being made on behalf of a limited company, a separate statement containing the names and addresses of all the directors of that company must be attached to the application form.

Schedule 1 of the Regulations made under the 1994 Act requires premises applying for approval to fulfil the following requirements:

- the premises must, in the opinion of the council, be a seemly and dignified venue for the solemnisation of marriages and what is considered seemly and dignified will be a question of fact based on what the premises are primarily used for, their situation, condition and state of repair;
- the premises must be regularly available to members of the public for use as a venue for the solemnisation of marriage;
- the premises must meet the standard of fire precautions as reasonably required by the council in consultation with the fire

# 10. THE LICENSING OF MARRIAGE VENUES

authority and also satisfy health and safety requirements for the welfare of visitors and employees;
- the premises must have no recent or active connection with any religion, religious practice or persuasion which would be incompatible with the use of the premises as a venue for civil marriage ceremonies;
- the room in which the marriage ceremony is to take place must be an identifiable and distinct part of the building.

Councils have a discretion to add their own requirements to the above such as that the room must be easily accessible by wheelchair users or that a room is made available for the registrar for at least one hour before the ceremony takes place.

The 1994 Act is intended to allow civil marriages to take place in venues such as stately homes, civic halls and other buildings without compromising the sanctity of marriage or the fundamental principles of English marriage law. Premises must be permanent and readily identifiable structures so that a marquee and most forms of transport would be unsuitable but a boat or vessel which is permanently moored might be considered suitable. For the same reason, wedding ceremonies cannot take place in an open air setting such as in a garden or in the grounds of a hotel. Unimpeded access to the premises must be available to allow members of the public to witness the marriage service and make objections before or during the ceremony. Private houses would not be considered a suitable venue as the public would not know them as a marriage venue or have unimpeded access to them. If the primary use of the building would bring the sanctity of marriage into disrepute then the premises will not be approved.

On receipt of the application and before any approval is granted, the council will make arrangements to inspect the premises and will also insert a notice in a newspaper circulating in the area requesting that any objections to the approval being granted are lodged with the council within three weeks. It is the council's responsibility to advertise the notice and the fee for it is included in the application fee.

The premises must satisfy local authority requirements for fire precautions and health and safety provision and copies of current health, safety and fire certificates must accompany the application together with copies of any other licence authorising the use of the premises for public entertainment or any other purposes.

The application form also requests information about the primary use the building is put to and the maximum number of people permitted to occupy the room intended for the marriage ceremony under the terms of the current fire certificate. A plan of the premises showing the room in which marriage ceremonies are to take place should be attached to the application form.

## The Registrars

Booking a registrar to perform the ceremony is a matter of liaison between the couple getting married, the manager of the approved premises and the registrar himself. Every registrar's office has its own system and the approved premises should not take bookings without checking that the registrar will be available on the day required. It is the couple's responsibility to arrange for the registrar to attend and they will have to pay his fee directly. This varies from area to area. In February 1997 it was £200 in Wiltshire. Two registrars must attend a civil marriage ceremony - one to officiate and one to record the ceremony. The fee however relates to each ceremony performed and not to each registrar.

## Religious Connections

Any building which has a continuing religious connection will be considered unsuitable as a venue for civil marriage ceremonies. Examples of a continuing religious connection are stained glass windows depicting religious scenes or symbols, a chapel in a stately home or a building which has fixtures or fittings associated with religious worship. If the primary use of the building is secular

# 10. THE LICENSING OF MARRIAGE VENUES

however a building in which a religious group only meet occasionally (such as a village hall) might be considered suitable.

Civil marriages conducted in this way can be followed by a celebration, blessing or commemoration of the couple's choice provided that it is not a religious marriage ceremony and is completely separate from the civil ceremony. If a religious blessing were to continually follow a civil ceremony at the premises this could be construed as a continuing religious connection and may result in the approval being revoked.

## Conditions

Schedule 2 of the Regulations gives standard conditions which must be attached to any approval granted which include the premises being available at all reasonable times for the council to inspect. The person who holds the approval must be responsible for ensuring that the conditions as required by law and the approving body are met. This can be done by appointing a person to be responsible for seeing that compliance takes place and that person's name and address notified to the council. Any changes made to the premises which alter its layout as shown in the plan submitted with the application for approval to the council must be notified to the county council immediately.

## Notices

A notice must be displayed at each public entrance to the premises for one hour before and for the duration of the marriage ceremony stating that the premises have been approved for the solemnisation of marriages in pursuance of s26(1)(bb) of the Marriage Act 1949. It must also identify and give directions to the room in which the marriage ceremony is being conducted. No charge can be made to the public for attending the ceremony.

Any notices which seek to advertise the premises as a potential venue for marriage ceremonies must not imply or state that the premises are recommended by the council.

## The Room

All marriage ceremonies must take place in the room identified on the plan submitted with the application. The arrangements and contents of the marriage ceremony must be approved in advance by the superintendent registrar for the district in which the premises are situated.

No food or drink can be consumed in the room for one hour before the ceremony or during it.

## Renewal

An approval lasts for a period of three years. Application to renew it can be made when the current approval has between six and twelve months left to run. Any application for renewal will extend the life of the current approval until the renewal has been determined. It will then run from the date of the expiry of the current approval. There is a fee for renewing an approval which varies from area to area.

## Revocation

An approval can be revoked if, after considering any representations made by the holder of that approval, the council considers that the structure or use of the premises has changed to such an extent that any of the conditions attached to it can no longer be met. The approval may also be revoked where the holder fails to comply with one or more of the standard or local conditions attached to it. Revocation may also be recommended by the Registrar General if he

# 10. THE LICENSING OF MARRIAGE VENUES

considers that there have been breaches of the laws relating to marriage.

## Reviews

Any applicant whose application for approval or its renewal is refused or who objects to local conditions being attached to the approval or who has his approval revoked can apply to the council for a review. This must be carried out by someone other than the person or body responsible for making the decision which is being objected to. The review panel will then confirm, rescind or vary the decision by imposing further or new conditions. Where the review is against a refusal to grant or renew an approval, or against the conditions attached to it, the council will charge a fee for the review taking place which is likely to be in the region of £200.

Where the Registrar General directs that an approval is revoked, the council does not have the power to review his decision.

## Records

The county council keeps a record of all approved premises in the area which is available for public inspection. The list of premises is also supplied to the superintendent registrar for the district in which the premises are situated and to the registrar general who will, from time to time, circulate the details to all superintendent registrars.

## Case Histories

• The owners of Raffles Country Hotel want to apply to the local county council for approval of their premises as a venue for civil marriage ceremonies. There is a room in the hotel which used to be a chapel when the building was a privately owned house which is where they intend to hold the ceremonies. They contact the council who send them an application form and notes for guidance on completing it. They fill it in and send with it a copy of their justices' licence, entertainment licence, fire and health and safety certificates, a detailed plan of the premises and the fee.

The chapel is currently being used as a staff changing room but the original stained glass windows were replaced with plain glass long before the current owners bought the hotel. On receiving the application, the council inspects the premises and after due consideration of all the facts, conclude that any religious connections the house might once have had have been severed. They are satisfied that the room is a distinct and identifiable part of the premises, that the premises themselves are a permanent and readily identifiable structure and with the primary use of the building. They inform the owners that the approval is granted.

•The owners of a stately home wish to hold civil marriage ceremonies beneath a rose bower in the grounds of the house. Their application is refused as there is no distinct, permanent and identifiable structure to approve. Licences cannot be granted for open air locations.

•The owners of a pleasure boat moored at Easton wish to hold civil marriage ceremonies on board. However they frequently use the boat in summer months to take parties of day trippers up and down the river and therefore the boat is not a permanent structure. The approval is refused but if the boat had been permanently moored it might have been granted.

# 11. PUBLIC ENTERTAINMENT AND COPYRIGHT MUSIC LICENCES

## Public Entertainment Licences

A public entertainment licence is needed where members of the public will be attending an event where music and dancing are to take place. A private function held by a club for the benefit of its members which is not open to the general public does not need such a licence.

*Karaoke* evenings are an example of events which require a licence if open to the public. Likewise, local amateur dramatics groups and schools need to obtain one before putting on a musical.

Application is made to the district council using one of their standard forms. In the Greater London area, the statutory body responsible is the relevant London borough council. The council will often require notice of the application to be published in the local paper and on the premises. Fees also vary and enquiries should be made of the council's licensing department.

The application form is fairly detailed and requests such information as what type of entertainment is to be held and the hours which it is to cover. If the application is general, for example where it is intended to have karaoke on some nights and live bands on others, the type of entertainment can be described on the form as "for all purposes". The form also asks whether the applicant is licensed to sell intoxicating liquor. If a licence is being applied for concurrently, this should be stated. The form also requires details of insurance for the premises and the electrical engineer responsible for carrying out routine inspections and an *inspection certificate* should be attached. The capacity of the premises for seating and standing customers and the number of staff must be stated. Once granted the licence may have conditions attached to it such as no admission or re-admission of persons after a specified time or that a doorman shall be on duty at all times when public entertainment is being held.

The council will consider the application by assessing the location of the premises, their suitability for music and dancing and if it is likely to cause a nuisance to neighbouring properties.

Fees can vary according to location but, for example, Kennet District Council in Devizes, Wiltshire currently charges £320 for a first licence if the applicant is a public house and £200 to renew one. A licence runs for one year.

## Case Histories

The fifth form of a comprehensive school want to stage a production of *The Boyfriend* at Christmas and serve warm punch in the interval. The school will need to apply for:

- a copyright music licence;
- an entertainment licence;
- an occasional permission (for the punch).

## Copyright Music

It should be remembered that most music "belongs" to somebody and that relaying it in a public place without first obtaining permission to do so is an infringement of that copyright. This applies whether it is playing music on a jukebox or where a TV or radio is provided in a bar. Whilst the person who originally broadcasts the music through television or radio will have the requisite copyright licence this does not cover the person relaying it. The transmission into the premises is considered a secondary and separate performance for which a copyright licence must be obtained.

All premises which use music require *Performing Rights Society (PRS) Public Performance Licences*. The PRS acts on behalf of the owners of music and collects the copyright dues on their behalf. This is done by issuing an annual licence to premises. The fee for such a licence varies according to the type and size of premises concerned and accordingly there are over forty different tariffs covering the

# 11. PUBLIC ENTERTAINMENT AND COPYRIGHT MUSIC

broadcast of music in places as diverse as hairdressing salons and airport lounges.

The PRS is a non-profit making body which pays out royalties from the monies it collects to the artists which belong to it and only deducts overheads from the monies collected. In addition the Society makes annual donations to musical causes such as awards and scholarships.

## The Tariffs

Tariff "P" is applied to music broadcast in public houses. It does not extend to music played in restaurants or dining rooms even if they are attached to the public house premises. These are the subject of a separate tariff.

The tariff is divided into standard and higher rates of royalties. Standard royalties are payable where a licence is obtained in advance of musical performances taking place. The higher tariff is applicable where musical performances commence before applying for a licence. In the second year however it is the standard tariff which applies, regardless of which level of royalty was payable in the first year.

The tariff varies according to the type of music played and whether that music is live or recorded.

The standard fee for a video juke box (December 1996) is £164.12 per annum but if the screen exceeds 66cm (26 ins) it increases to £196.24 per annum.

Royalties are also due for television broadcasts whether it is terrestrial, satellite or cable, radios, music centres, background music, karaoke performances and music quizzes where musical performances form a major part of the quiz and live entertainment. Royalties for the performance of live music are calculated by taking a percentage of the amount the premises spend on live music per year and by considering the audience capacity of the building.

All royalties are subject to VAT at the prevailing rate.

Tariff "SP" applies to small premises and is effective from November 1996. Small premises are those with a maximum of thirty seats such as doctors and dentists waiting rooms and hairdressing salons.

Tariff "HR" applies to hotels, restaurants and cafes, fast food outlets, function rooms, banqueting suites and boarding and guest houses. A licence is required where music is either performed live, relayed as background music in bedrooms or corridors or through television, radio, juke boxes, music centres or cassette recorders.

Higher and standard royalty rates apply and the licence fee for live musical performances is calculated as a percentage of the annual expenditure on live music and audience or function capacity.

Where discos are held at dances or dinners, the standard royalty rate is £5.46 per function for the first 100 persons and £1.38 for each further group of twenty-five persons.

Where a mixture of live and recorded music is broadcast these rates will apply unless the annual expenditure on live music exceeds £8,035 in which case the standard royalty is calculated at 4% of that annual expenditure.

Where a hotel has fifteen letting bedrooms or less and restricts the use of its facilities to residential guests, the annual licence fee for TV, radio, records, tapes, CD's, music centres, video recorders and background music is limited to a standard annual royalty of £68.34.

If the premises are open for less than twenty-six weeks in the licensing year the royalties due on the above are reduced by a third subject to a minimum annual royalty of £54.69.

A PRS licence is needed in addition to a television licence or a local authority entertainments licence. The owner or manager of the premises should assume responsibility for obtaining the licence.

The Performing Rights Society has a phone line (0345 581 868) to help with queries and provide application forms and tariff information. In addition there are PRS offices throughout the country who are always willing to help with queries.

## Phonographic Performance Licences

A Phonographic Performance Licence (PPL) is required in addition to any licence granted by the Performing Rights Society.

# 11. PUBLIC ENTERTAINMENT AND COPYRIGHT MUSIC

Two copyrights are involved whenever music is played in public, the first belonging to the record producer or record company (PPL licence) and the second to the composer or music publisher (PRS licence).

Phonographic Performance Limited was set up by the record industry to grant licences to anyone wishing to play records, tapes, cassettes or CD's in public. Owning a record, tape, cassette or CD does not confer automatic rights to broadcast them in public.

PPL looks after the interests of over 12,000 different record companies and the revenue generated from its licence fees is distributed to artists and record companies.

Tapes, records. CD's and cassettes that are played in bars, clubs, hotels or nightclubs therefore require a licence. This applies wherever there is a public performance of the music, even in a private members club. A wedding reception on the other hand, which takes place in a public hall hired for the occasion, is considered a private performance and no licence is required. Additionally certain bodies such as charitable organisations do not need licences.

A PPL licence usually lasts for a period of one year although one off licences can be granted for special events. The fee for a licence will depend on how many hours of music is broadcast, the type of establishment concerned and whether the music is background music or used in a specific way such as music played at a disco or dance, and the average attendance at those premises.

Licence fees are set by tariffs and as at September 1996 the fee for background music only in a public house, hotel or bar is £67.55 plus VAT per annum.

# 12. BETTING OFFICE LICENCES

## Introduction

Betting licences are granted by a committee of justices which form the Betting Licensing Committee and, as such, convene on specified days in January, April, July and October to consider applications. Notice of the days on which the committee will consider applications for and renewals of bookmakers' permits, betting agency permits and betting office licences will be advertised in a newspaper circulating in the district for which the committee have jurisdiction.

Only the following are entitled to apply for a betting shop licence:
- the current holder of a bookmakers permit or someone applying for one;
- the Totalizator Board;
- someone who is accredited by a bookmaker holding a permit or by the Totalisator Board, as an agent for receiving or negotiating bets in the course of his business for the person who will place his bet with that bookmaker or Totalisator Board and who is a holder of or applying for a betting agency permit.

## Bookmaker's Permits

A bookmaker's permit is granted by a body of magistrates to enable a person to carry on business as a bookmaker whether he is involved in betting on a race course, dog track or in a licensed betting office. The procedure for obtaining a permit is similar to that for obtaining a betting shop licence.

## Betting Agency Permits

A betting agency permit authorises the holder to have a betting office licence and is granted by the same body of magistrates.

## 12. BETTING OFFICE LICENCES

### Applying for a Betting Office Licence

Application is made to the clerk to the justices for the area in which the premises are situated (see *Form 9* on page 117). While an application can be made at any time, it can only be considered on those days set aside by the magistrates for considering such applications.

### Notices

No later than seven days after applying for a betting office licence a copy of the application must be sent to the chief officer of Police for the area in which the premises are situated and also to the local authority and the collector for Customs & Excise in the area.

A notice giving details of the application must be displayed outside the entrance to the premises applying for the licence no later than fourteen days after the application has been sent to the magistrates.

Within fourteen days of making the application, a notice must be placed in a newspaper circulating in the area stating that anyone wishing to object to the licence being granted must send, by a date specified within the notice, but no earlier than fourteen days after the date the notice appears in the paper, two copies of a statement of objections to the clerk to the justices and include their address.

The applicant must then send a copy of the newspaper notice to the justices no later than seven days after publication. The justices are unable to consider the application earlier than fourteen days after the date for objections published in the newspaper notice. No earlier than seven days before the date appointed for the consideration of the application or earlier than the date stated in the newspaper notice, the clerk to the magistrates should send written notice of the date, time and place where the application is to be considered to:

- the applicant;
- the chief officer of Police;
- any objector who has made written objections which are not withdrawn by that time and who has included his address with his objections;
- the collector for Customs & Excise in the area

A notice detailing the arrangements for the meeting must also be displayed at the place where the magistrates are to convene to consider the application in such a way that it can be easily read by the public.

If no objections have been received, or any that have been made have been withdrawn before the application is considered, then the application will take place without a formal hearing and without the applicant needing to attend. If a hearing does take place, then both the applicant and objectors will be able to make representations. The applicant may represent himself or instruct a solicitor. At any hearing that takes place, the applicant or his representative will be asked to swear on oath and give a brief background to the application. One of the things he must show in his submissions to the magistrates is that there is a demand in the area where the premises are situated for a betting shop. He can call on any witnesses he may have brought along with him to vouch for this. It is a good idea to take a plan of the premises to the hearing showing both the location of the premises and its internal design. A telephone call to the magistrates' clerk beforehand will identify precisely what type of plans they require as requirements can vary from area to area.

At the hearing the justices have the power to make an order as to who should pay the costs of the application. This may be that the applicant pays the objector's costs or vice versa.

## Refusal of a Betting Office Licence

The magistrates must refuse to grant a betting office licence if they are not satisfied:

## 12. BETTING OFFICE LICENCES

- that the applicant will be the holder of a bookmaker's licence or betting agency permit on the date the licence is due to come into effect;
- that the premises are not or will not be enclosed;
- that there is no access between the premises and the street other than through other premises which are not a part of the betting shop.

They may refuse the application where they consider:

- that the premises are not suitable for use as a licensed betting office because of their layout, condition, location or character;
- that there is insufficient demand in the area to merit a betting office being set up.

If they refuse to grant a license, the magistrates must state their grounds for doing so and notify the applicant accordingly. The applicant then has twenty-one days from the date of receiving the notice of refusal in which to make an appeal to the Crown Court. Neither the Police nor any objector has the right to appeal against a licence being granted.

Any notice of appeal completed by the applicant is sent to the magistrates' clerk who sends it on to the Crown Court together with a statement as to why the application was refused and a list of the names and addresses of the objectors present at the application. The Crown Court then sends seven days' notice of the date, time and place of the appeal to the appellant, the Police, Customs & Excise and any person who appeared at the application as an objector and also to the magistrates who refused the application.

At the hearing of the appeal, the Crown Court will either confirm the refusal or grant or renew the application upon payment by the appellant of the appropriate fee. The decision of the Crown Court is final.

## Renewing a Betting Office Licence

A betting office licence will contain details of the date it is to come into effect and will normally cease to be effective from the 31 May which falls not less than three and no more than fifteen months after the date the licence becomes operative.

In February of each year the magistrates responsible for betting office licence applications are required to notify all licence holders whose licences are due for renewal in the coming year. Additionally they will place a notice in the newspaper stating the dates on which they will be meeting to consider applications for renewals.

The notice sent to the holder of the licence due for renewal will ask him to make his application to renew his licence before a certain specified date which must not be earlier than fourteen days following receipt of the notice being sent and appearing in the newspaper.

The newspaper notice must state that any person wishing to object to the renewal of any particular licence must send before a date specified and no earlier than fourteen days after that notice is published, two copies of a written statement containing the grounds of objection to the clerk to the justices at a given address (see *Form 10* on page 117)

No earlier than the date specified in the newspaper notice and no later than seven days before the date set aside for the consideration of renewal applications, the magistrates' clerk must send any objector notification as to whether or not an application for renewal of the licence he is objecting to has been received. The clerk must also send the person applying for renewal copies of any objections received from the Police, local authority or any other person who has not withdrawn such objections before that date.

The grounds for refusing to renew a betting office licence are the same as those for refusing to grant one. In addition however, the magistrates may refuse to renew a betting office licence where they have reason to believe that the premises have failed to be properly conducted under the terms of the licence granted.

There is also a right of appeal to the Crown Court and the procedure is the same as for appealing against a refusal to grant a licence. If the magistrates refuse to renew a licence then the licence

## 12. BETTING OFFICE LICENCES

remains in force until the end of the period allowed for making an appeal and continues in force until any appeal is determined or abandoned.

## Death of a Licence Holder

If a licence holder dies the licence will remain in force for a period of six months from the date of his death. His personal representatives will then be deemed to be the licence holders. The six month period may be extended by the personal representatives applying to the magistrates and may be extended if the magistrates are satisfied that such an extension is necessary for the purposes of winding up the estate of the deceased and where no other circumstances exist to make such an extension undesirable.

# 13. GAMING

## Gaming

Section 2 of the Gaming Act 1968 forbids gaming other than on licensed or registered premises where any one or more of the following conditions are fulfilled:

- the game involves playing or staking a claim against a bank whether or not that bank is held by one or more of the players;
- the nature of the game is such that the chances taken in it are not equally favourable to all those players taking part;
- the nature of the game is such that the chances between the player and the person he plays with are not equally favourable.

Therefore games which involve using a bank and are not of equal chance can only be played on licensed or registered premises. Where such games take place on private premises however, they are not prohibited altogether provided that the gaming is not being carried on in the course of trade or business. In such circumstances the players must be exclusively or mostly residents at those premises.

Members clubs must be registered in order to host such games and proprietary clubs operating gaming with a commercial or profitable element must be licensed. The difference between the two is that in a members club, the members all have an equal share in the ownership of all the property. In a proprietary club the property belongs to the proprietor and members are allowed to use the premises and property in return for paying a subscription.

## Application

An application for a gaming licence is made in two parts. Firstly, the consent of the Gaming Board for Great Britain, which regulates

# 13. GAMING

gaming in this country, must be obtained. The second part is applying to the magistrates for the gaming licence itself.

## Consent by the Gaming Board

Consent is given in the form of a certificate which allows a person to apply for a gaming licence for a specified set of premises. Applying for this certificate is known as a consent application. The consent application must:

- be made by the person intending to apply for the licence;
- specify the premises for which the licence is being sought;
- specify whether the licence is to be for a bingo club only.

The Board will supply the applicant with the relevant form on which to make the consent application and supply guidelines to assist the applicant with completing it. The Board will not issue a certificate where the applicant is under twenty-one, or not resident in Great Britain for the six months before he application. An application may be granted if made by a British registered company.

The Board will consider the application by assessing whether:

- the gaming on the premises will be fairly and properly conducted;
- the applicant is likely to be capable of and diligent in ensuring that the provisions of the Gaming Act and the regulations made under it will be strictly adhered to and complied with;
- the premises will be operated without disorder or disturbance;
- the character, reputation and financial status of the applicant and any person who would be appointed to manage it or for whose benefit the club would be operated is satisfactory;
- any other circumstances it considers relevant.

Once granted the certificate will specify the name of the applicant, the premises concerned, whether the consent is limited to an application for a bingo club licence or not and the time within which the licence application must be made.

If the Board raise objections about granting a certificate, they must supply the applicant with sufficient information to allow him to answer them. If they refuse to grant a certificate they do not have to state their reasons for doing so.

## Applying for a Gaming Licence

The second part of the procedure is to apply for the licence itself. Application is made to the same body of magistrates who are responsible for granting betting office licences. The application is made to the clerk to the justices for the area in which the premises are situated.

The application must state by name and description a club which is already in existence or which is to come into existence for the purposes of which the licence is being sought. The application must be accompanied by a copy of the Board's certificate of consent and these are sent to the clerk to the justices for the area in which the premises are situated.

No later than seven days after the date on which the application is sent to the court a copy must be sent to:

- The Gaming Board;
- The chief officer of Police for the area in which the premises are situated;
- The appropriate local authority (or London borough council);
- The appropriate fire authority, if separate from the above;
- The Collector of Customs & Excise for the area in which the premises are situated.

## Notices

Within fourteen days of sending the application to the court, a notice must be inserted in a newspaper circulating in the district in which the premises are or are to be situated. This notice must state:

# 13. GAMING

- The name of the person applying for the licence;
- The name of the club and its location;
- Whether the licence is to be for a bingo club or other licence.

It must also specify the date by which any person wishing to object must do so by sending two copies of their written objections to the clerk to the justices at a given address. This date must not be earlier than fourteen days after the newspaper notice is published.

No later than fourteen days before the date so specified in the newspaper notice the applicant must also display a notice giving the same information outside his premises and keep it displayed until the date by which objections must be received has expired. It must not contain any information other than that required by the Gaming Act.

Within seven days of the notice appearing in the newspaper, the applicant must send a copy of that newspaper to the clerk to the justices. The justices cannot consider the application any earlier than fourteen days after the date specified in the newspaper notice.

After this date has passed, but not later than seven days before the date fixed by the magistrates for considering the application, the clerk to the justices will send out written notice of the time date and place when the application is to be heard. This must be sent to:

- the applicant;
- the Gaming Board;
- the Police;
- the local authority;
- the fire authority;
- the collector for Customs & Excise for the area;
- objectors who have not withdrawn their objections.

A notice must also be displayed at the place the meeting is to be held in such a way that it can be easily read by the public.

## The Licence

If no objections have been received or those received have been withdrawn, the magistrates will consider the licence without a formal hearing. Otherwise those permitted to attend the application are the applicant, objectors who have not withdrawn their objections and any person who objects out of time who the magistrates agree to hear. The magistrates must also hear any representations made by or on behalf of the Gaming Board, the Police, the local authority, the fire authority or the Commissioners of Customs & Excise. Evidence is given on oath and the magistrates have the power to order the applicant to pay any objector's costs or vice versa if they consider it appropriate.

## Refusing to Grant a Licence

The magistrates may refuse to grant a licence if they are not satisfied that a demand for gaming facilities exists in the area. If it is shown that such a demand does exist however they may still refuse to grant the licence if they consider that there are already sufficient gaming facilities in the area to meet the demand. As demand is the most common ground for refusing to grant a licence, the applicant should attempt to show that there is either a demand for gaming facilities within the area because no other such facilities exist or those that do exist fail to meet it.

The magistrates may also refuse to grant a licence, whether or not the question of demand is satisfied, where they consider:
- that the premises are unsuitable because of their location, layout, character or condition;
- that the applicant is not a fit and proper person to hold a gaming licence;
- that if a licence was granted the club would either be managed by or operated for the benefit of a person other than the applicant who would be refused a gaming licence should he apply of his own accord because he would not be considered a fit and proper person to hold such a licence.

The justices may also refuse to grant a licence where:

# 13. GAMING

- the magistrates, the Police, the local authority, fire authority or their authorised representatives have been refused reasonable access to inspect the premises;
- duty payable under the gaming laws (including bingo duty) remains unpaid;
- the premises are designed in such a way that a person might gain access directly to them from private premises not included in the licence which includes courtyards, passages and stairways;
- where the licence is for premises situated wholly or partly outside the area specified in the Gaming Clubs (Permitted Areas) Regulations 1971 - in such circumstances the justices must refuse to grant or renew a licence for hard gaming in areas where it is prohibited by law.

## Restrictions

On granting a licence the magistrates may impose restrictions limiting its operation and effect as follows:

- the hours during which gaming is permitted;
- limiting gaming to specified parts of the premises;
- limiting gaming to certain types of games;
- limiting the purposes for which the premises may be used other than gaming.

Where a certificate of consent issued by the Gaming Board limits that consent to a bingo club licence, then when granting or renewing the licence to which that consent relates, the magistrates must add restrictions to it which limit the gaming on those premises to bingo only. In such circumstances, no additional restrictions limiting the other activities which may be held on the premises can be added as the Gaming Act aims to encourage bingo clubs to run other forms of entertainment in addition to bingo.

Any restrictions imposed are effective until the licence expires or is renewed.

In applications other than those for bingo club licences, the magistrates must impose restrictions on the licence limiting gaming to games other than bingo and impose restrictions limiting the other purposes for which the premises may be used. These will usually exclude music, dancing and live entertainment as such mixed use is considered to attract members of the public to gaming by the provision of other entertainment and the Gaming Act actively seeks to discourage this.

The Gaming Board advises the magistrates throughout the application as to whether to impose restrictions and provides information about the demand by players for gaming facilities within the area in question. The applicant is entitled to request that the magistrates provide him with a statement of any advice provided by the Board which they propose to rely on when determining the licensing application.

## Appeals

Where the magistrates refuse to grant or renew a licence or attach restrictions to it, their clerk must notify the applicant accordingly. The applicant can then appeal against the decision by sending notice of his intention to do so to the magistrates' clerk. He must do this within twenty-one days of receiving the notice. The magistrates' clerk will then forward it on to the Crown Court together with a statement of the decision being appealed against and a list of the names and addresses of the appellant and any objectors present at the application. The Crown Court must give no less than fourteen days' notice of the date time and place on which the appeal is to be heard to the Gaming Board, the applicant, the Police, Customs & Excise, the magistrates who refused to renew/grant the licence or who attached restrictions and any objectors who were present at the original application. The Crown Court may allow, dismiss, reverse or vary any part of the decision made by the magistrates whether or not the appeal relates to the part reversed or varied or not. The decision of the Crown Court is final and it can make orders in relation to the costs of the appeal where it consider just to do so.

# 13. GAMING

The Gaming Board may also lodge an appeal where it considers that a licence should not have been granted or renewed or where it considers that restrictions should have been attached to it.

## Renewal

A licence ceases to be effective one year after it was granted or renewed. The procedure for renewing a gaming licence is the same as applying for a new licence except that no notice need be displayed on the club premises and it is the magistrates' clerk's responsibility to advertise notice of the intention to renew in the newspaper.

Application to renew must be made no earlier than five and no later than three months before the licence is due to expire. A licence can however be renewed at a later date where the magistrates are satisfied with the reasons given for failing to renew it on time.

At the application for renewal, restrictions may be continued or added and the right of appeal and procedure is the same as for the grant of a new licence.

## Revocation of a Certificate of Consent

The Gaming Board can revoke a certificate of consent at any time whether or not a licence has already been granted, where certain specified situations arise as follows:

- if the holder of the certificate was to apply for a certificate at that time the Board would not issue one to him because he was either under twenty-one years of age, not resident in Great Britain for the previous six months or is a body corporate not registered in Great Britain;
- that information given in relation to the certificate being issued by or behalf of the applicant was false in whole or in part;
- that since the certificate was issued a licence issued to the holder of that certificate in respect of the same or different premises has been cancelled by a disqualification order;

- that gaming on the premises is being operated by someone other than the holder of the certificate of consent and that person is someone to whom the Board would not issue a certificate.

Where it is decided to revoke a certificate, notice must be served on the certificate holder stating that revocation of the certificate will take place eight weeks from the date on which the notice is received. Revoking a certificate will render any gaming licence held ineffective.

## Cancellation

Anyone may apply at any time for a licence to be cancelled by applying to the magistrates on a standard form accompanied by two copies of a statement setting out the grounds on which the application to cancel is being made. When this is received by the magistrates' clerk, he will pass it on to one of the magistrates to consider. If that magistrate feels that the matters raised should wait and be heard at the date on which the licence is due for renewal or ought to have been raised when the licence was granted or renewed previously, then he must notify the applicant accordingly that the application is refused but that he may raise the matters contained within it as objections at the subsequent application for renewal.

If the magistrate considers that the application should be dealt with at once he must refer it to the other magistrates who will set a time for the application to be heard and notify the time, date and place of the hearing to:

- the applicant applying for the cancellation;
- the holder of the licence;
- the Police;
- Customs & Excise;
- The Gaming Board.

Such notice must be given to the above no less than twenty-one days before the date of the hearing. The licence holder must also be

# 13. GAMING

sent a copy of the statement containing the grounds of the application to cancel the licence.

At the hearing the magistrates will consider the application and the applicant and licence holder are entitled to make representations if they wish to do so, either in person or through their solicitor or barrister. Evidence is given on oath and the magistrates may order that the costs of the application are paid either by the licence holder or the applicant as they consider appropriate.

The magistrates must refuse to cancel the licence where they feel that the application has been brought on grounds that ought properly to have been raised by way of objections when the licence was either granted or previously renewed. Otherwise they may cancel a licence for the same reasons as they would refuse to grant or renew one.

There is a right of appeal against any decision to cancel the licence and the procedure is the same as for an appeal against a refusal to grant or renew a licence.

If the magistrates decide to cancel a licence, the licence will remain in force until the time allowed for making an appeal has expired or the appeal has been determined or abandoned. If the magistrates refuse to cancel a licence, and the Gaming Board considers that it should be cancelled, it has a right of appeal to the Crown Court.

## Convictions

A licence can be cancelled where the licence holder is convicted of certain statutory offences. This can happen where there is a second or subsequent conviction for an offence committed in relation to gaming on the licensed premises while that licence has been held by the same person. Customs & Excise will apply in such circumstances for the licence to be cancelled and the magistrates must then order its cancellation.

When a licence is cancelled in this way, the clerk to the magistrates responsible for the cancellation, must send a copy of the cancellation order to the clerk to the magistrates responsible for gaming licence matters in the area in which the licensed premises are situated unless the magistrates are one and the same. The magistrates who deal with gaming licences for the area in which the premises are situated must then refuse any application made by the licence holder in respect of the same or any other premises which is made within twelve months of the date of the cancellation order. Notification of the cancellation must also be sent to the Gaming Board.

## Disqualification Orders

Where a licence is cancelled by the magistrates, they have a discretion to make a disqualification order prohibiting a gaming licence being held by the premises for a specified period of time which must not exceed five years from the date the cancellation order came into effect.

The licence holder has a right of appeal to the Crown Court against the cancellation and subsequent disqualification order.

A disqualification order may also be made by a court which convicts a licence holder of contravening sections 24 and 25 of the Gaming Act 1968 which relate to contravention of the rules of gaming. Any such disqualification order made under these provisions prohibits a licence being held for the premises where the offence was committed for a specified period not in excess of five years from the date the disqualification order came into effect. Any licence obtained before the disqualification order came into effect is cancelled from that date.

In both cases, disqualification will not come into effect until the time allowed for making an appeal has elapsed or if an appeal is made, until that appeal is determined or abandoned.

Application can be made during the disqualification period for the disqualification order to be varied or revoked by altering the duration of the disqualification order. A copy of any such application must be sent to the chief officer of Police for the area. Such applications are made to the magistrates' court even if the disqualification order was made by the Crown Court.

# 13. GAMING

## Death of a Licence Holder

If the licence holder dies, the licence will continue in force until six months has expired from the date of death. The deceased's personal representatives are deemed to be the holders of the licence except for the purposes of renewing it. The six month period may be extended if the magistrates are satisfied that an extension is necessary for the purposes of winding up the estate of the deceased where no other circumstances exist to make such an extension undesirable.

## Transferring a Gaming Licence

A gaming licence can be transferred from one person to another but not from one set of premises to another. Before making an application for a transfer the licence holder must obtain a further certificate of consent from the Gaming Board. They can refuse to issue one for the same reasons as they can refuse in respect of a gaming licence. When assessing whether to allow an application to be made for a licence to be transferred the Gaming Board will consider:

- whether the person to whom the licence is to be transferred is likely to be capable of and diligent in securing the provisions of the Gaming Act 1968 and any provisions made under it;
- whether gaming on the premises will be fairly and properly conducted;
- whether the premises will be operated without disorder and disturbance;
- the financial standing, reputation and character of the person to whom the licence is to be transferred and that of any person who would maintain the club if the licence were transferred or for whose benefit the club would operated;
- any other matters considered relevant.

Any certificate that is issued will state a time within which the application for a transfer must be made to the magistrates. The

Gaming Board has the power to revoke its consent at any time before such an application is made but only where it has reason to believe that the information supplied to them, and forming a basis on which the consent was granted, was false. The Gaming Board may also cancel the certificate of consent where a licence is subsequently cancelled by a disqualification order.

Applications for transfers are made to the magistrates with the authority to deal with gaming matters in the area. They must be accompanied by the certificate of consent from the Gaming Board and a copy of the application must be sent to the Gaming Board, the Police, the local authority and Customs & Excise within seven days of sending the application to the magistrates.

## Refusing a Transfer

The magistrates can only refuse to grant the transfer where they consider:

- that the person to whom the licence is to be transferred is not a fit and proper person to hold a gaming licence;
- that if the licence were transferred to that person, the club would be managed or carried on for the benefit of a person who, if he applied for a gaming licence himself, would be refused on the basis that he was not a fit and proper person to hold the licence;
- that duties payable by law remain unpaid.

If the magistrates refuse to grant the transfer, the applicant may appeal to the Crown Court. Where the Gaming Board opposes a transfer but it is granted by the magistrates, it too can appeal.

## Gaming Licence Fees

Gaming licences can only be granted, renewed or transferred upon the payment of a statutory fee. As these are amended by statute from time to time it is advisable to make enquiries of individual areas.

# 13. GAMING

## Companies Holding Gaming Licences

Where a gaming licence is held by a company or other corporate body, and there is a change in the directors of that company or corporate body or in those who the directors act on behalf of, notice of such changes must be sent to the Gaming Board, the clerk to the magistrates and the Police.

## Relinquishing a Gaming Licence

The holder of a gaming licence can relinquish it altogether by serving notice on the magistrates' clerk. The licence will then be considered cancelled. It is the clerk's responsibility to serve notice of the cancellation on the Gaming Board, the Police, the local authority, fire authority and Customs & Excise.

## Fruit Machine Licences

If a "fruit machine" is used on premises it is necessary to have a *section 34 gaming licence*. Where premises are licensed to sell alcoholic beverages under the terms of a justices' licence, application for a gaming licence is made to the licensing justices. For premises which are unlicensed, or hold a restaurant, residential or combined restaurant and residential licence, application is made to the local authority.

An application form for unlicensed premises can be obtained from the local district council. The current fee for a gaming licence is £32 and lasts for three years. In addition gaming machine licence duty is payable to Customs & Excise.

Two fruit or gaming machines are allowed per set of premises although amusement arcades are allowed more.

For licensed premises application is made to the magistrates' court and application forms can obtained from Shaw and Sons (01322 550676) as some licensing departments of the court do not provide

99

them. The form should be completed and sent to the licensing section of the local magistrates' court with the fee and a plan of the premises which shows where the gaming machines are to be situated.

## Bingo Licences

Bingo clubs are distinguished from other gaming clubs by the provisions of the Gaming Act 1968 and a licence for a bingo club is a gaming licence with restrictions attached to it limiting its operation to the playing of bingo only.

The other difference between gaming clubs and those licensed to play bingo on their premises, is that a person, in general gaming clubs can only take part in the gaming as a member where more than forty-eight hours have elapsed since applying for membership or where written notice is given at the premises of his intention to take part in the gaming. A member of a bingo club on the other hand may join in the activities after twenty-four hours have elapsed since applying for membership. Application for membership does not have to be made in person at the bingo club premises.

Section 12(1) of the Gaming Act 1968 states that no person can participate in gaming if he is not on the premises at the time the gaming takes place but allows for linked and multiple games of bingo. Linked bingo is played simultaneously on different sets of premises and multiple bingo is played jointly on different sets of premises.

For multiple bingo the maximum playing prize is £50,000 and the organiser of the game must be certificated by the Gaming Board. Only one game of multiple bingo may be played in any one twenty four hour period with the game not exceeding thirty minutes.

For linked bingo there is a limit of £3,500 paid out as the total prize money in any one week although this can be varied by regulation (see *Form 11* on page 118).

# 14. GAMING: MEMBERS CLUBS

## Registration

Members' clubs which provide gaming are required to be registered rather than licensed. Application for registration is made to the magistrates' clerk with authority for gaming licence matters in the area in which the premises are situated. The application must specify by name and by description the premises which are currently being used or intended to be used by the club. The application for registration is made in the same way as an application for a gaming licence with the following exceptions:

- a certificate of consent does not have to be obtained beforehand from the Gaming Board;
- the newspaper notice does not need to state whether the application is for a bingo licence or general gaming licence;
- no notice need be displayed on the premises to be used for gaming in advance of the application;
- no notice need be given to the fire and local authorities.

A copy of the application must be sent to the Gaming Board. Renewal of a club's registration follows the same procedure as an application to renew a gaming licence.

## Refusal

The magistrates must refuse to register or renew a club's registration if they consider that the club is not a bona fide members club, has less than twenty-five members or is only temporary in character. They must also refuse to register or renew a club's registration if they consider that the principal purpose for establishing or operating the club is for gaming rather than providing gaming as a subsidiary

# THE LICENSING HANDBOOK

activity for its members. The exception is where gaming consists entirely of playing bridge or whist or a combination of both.

A refusal may occur where, having previously been registered, the club's registration is cancelled or the club is refused a renewal of its registration. The magistrates may refuse to renew a registration where:

- a person has been convicted of an offence under the Gaming Act 1968;
- the premises have been conducted in a disorderly manner which has caused disturbance;
- gaming on the premises permitted by registration has been conducted dishonestly;
- the registered premises have been used for an unlawful purpose or as a resort for prostitutes and criminals, when the magistrates *must* refuse renewal;
- bingo duty remains unpaid the magistrates must refuse to renew a registration.

## Restrictions on Registration

The magistrates may impose restrictions at an application for registration or renewal limiting gaming to certain parts of the club's premises only.

## Appeals

The magistrates' clerk must notify the party applying for registration of any refusal by the magistrates to register or renew registration or where the magistrates impose restrictions. Within twenty-one days of receiving such notice, the applicant may appeal to the Crown Court by sending notice of his intention to do so to the magistrates' clerk who will then forward it to the Crown Court together with a note of the decision being appealed against and the names and addresses of the applicant and any objectors. The Crown Court will then give no

# 14. GAMING: MEMBERS CLUBS

less than fourteen days' notice of the date, time and place when the appeal is to be heard to the applicant, the Gaming Board, the Police, Customs & Excise and any person who opposed the registration or renewal of registration. The Crown Court may dismiss or vary the magistrates' decision and their decision is final. The Gaming Board also has a right of appeal to the Crown Court where registration or renewal is allowed by the magistrates and where they consider that it should have been refused.

## Cancellation of Registration

A registration may be refused or cancelled on the same grounds as a gaming licence may be refused or cancelled and for the same reasons.

If a person is convicted of an offence under the Gaming Act 1968 or in contravention of the Regulations made under it and Customs & Excise certify that the offence is a second or subsequent one for such an offence committed in relation to gaming on the premises and apply to the court for an order cancelling registration, then the magistrates must cancel it. This is the case whether the offence has been committed by the same or different persons.

Where the magistrates decide to cancel a registration, their clerk must give notice to the chairman or secretary of the club concerned who may then send a notice of appeal to the magistrates' clerk for an appeal to be heard in the Crown Court. This must be done within twenty-one days of receiving the notice of intended cancellation. The order cancelling registration will not take effect until the period allowed for lodging an appeal has expired or, if an appeal is made, until that appeal has been determined or abandoned. If the appeal is allowed the order will not have any effect at all and if it is allowed, a copy of it must be sent to the magistrates with jurisdiction for club registration in the area in which the premises in question are situated if these are a different body from those who make the cancellation order. These magistrates must then refuse to allow registration of the club concerned if it applies for registration for the same or any other premises within twelve months of the date of the cancellation order coming in to effect.

## Registration Certificates

Where a club is registered for gaming, the magistrates must issue a standard registration certificate which must state any restrictions imposed on the registration. A registration certificate ceases to be effective one year from the date it is granted if it is not renewed before that time. An application for the certificate to be renewed can specify a length of time the applicant wishes the certificate to run for and this can be a period of time not exceeding ten years. If no specific time is stated then the renewal will last a year from the date of renewal. Where the magistrates refuse to allow a renewal the registration certificate ceases to be effective upon the expiry of the time allowed for making an appeal or until any appeal made is determined or abandoned.

## Relinquishing Registration

If a club wishes to cease its registration for gaming it can send a notice to the magistrates' clerk at any time. The registration will then be treated as cancelled and it is the magistrates' clerk's responsibility to notify the Gaming Board, the Police and Customs & Excise accordingly.

## Restrictions on Games Played

Bankers' games and games which are not of equal chance may not be played on licensed or registered premises but regulations can be made which allow gaming of this type if such a game is one of those specified in regulations made under the Gaming Act which are varied from time to time. Under these Regulations any such gaming is

## 14. GAMING: MEMBERS CLUBS

required to be carried out in strict accordance with the conditions set out in those Regulations. Regulations made in 1970, for example, permit roulette, dice, baccarat and blackjack to be played on licensed premises in accordance with the gaming rules laid down in those Regulations. Casino stud poker is one of the games recently allowed by Regulation to be played in gaming clubs.

# 15. LEGAL RIGHTS IN RESTAURANTS

## Introduction

Customers do complain in restaurants, sometimes justifiably sometimes not. While resorting to a formal assertion of legal rights is rarely the best way of resolving a dispute in this kind of situation, it is advisable for both customer and restauranteur to know where they stand in relation to the law.

## The Food

There are certain standards that can be expected of the food served in restaurants and of the restaurant itself. The food served must be fit for its purpose and comply with the description given to it. It must be of a quality reasonably to be expected of an establishment of its kind. The wine should be served at the correct temperature. Likewise the cutlery, crockery or glasses should not be chipped or dirty.

A customer who takes more than a few mouthfuls of food will be taken as accepting the meal and will have to pay for it. If dissatisfied on tasting or inspecting it, he should complain at once.

A customer should expect a reasonable standard of food, presentation and service and a waiter should attend the table within a few minutes of the customer being seated at his table if only to offer a drink. If a waiter spills soup or a drink over a customer, the restaurant should bear the dry cleaning cost if it is more than just a splash.

The time that a customer waits for his food will obviously depend on the type of establishment and the food that it provides. Some restaurants include a notice on the menus stating that fresh food takes longer to prepare.

# 15. LEGAL RIGHTS IN RESTAURANTS

## "Waiter, there's a Fly in my Soup..."

Usually a quiet word in the waiter's ear will be sufficient to rectify the situation. If it does not, and the food and service do not improve, or if the food arrives and the gammon steak is tougher than a sheepskin glove or the meat is cooked to a frazzle, then the manager should be informed immediately. If the customer intends to leave it to the end of the meal to complain, the restaurant may claim that he is making a fuss to avoid payment.

If the food does not improve as dinner progresses, this should be made clear to the manager and the customer should only offer to pay what he considers to be a reasonable price for the meals he has been given when he receives the bill. If not paying the full amount the customer must offer to provide his name and address. A customer should not walk out simply without paying as he could later be accused of the criminal offence of making off without payment. Theoretically a customer could pay the bill and then bring a claim in the county court to recover the difference between what was paid and what the meal was worth. Once people get home and a few days have passed most will probably decide not to bother and in any event, going down this avenue may cost more than the meal did in the first place.

Most restaurants will however deduct part of the price of a meal from the bill as a gesture of goodwill.

## The Police

In some cases the management may prove less than obliging and may threaten to call the Police if a customer refuses to pay. The Police will normally regard this as a civil dispute and none of their concern. They will only become involved if there is a breach of the peace so it is important for everybody to stay calm! If the restauranteur does call the Police, the customer should wait for them to arrive and explain that he is not trying to get out of paying but simply exercising his rights under the civil law to deduct money from the bill.

If when a customer refuses to pay for a meal which he found inedible and the restaurant tries to threaten or detain him against his will, that could constitute false imprisonment, which is both a criminal and civil wrong.

## "There's a Rat in the Kitchen..."

If the complaint is to do with the general hygiene of the premises, the establishment should be reported to the local environmental health officer. If someone suspects that he has suffered food poisoning as a result of eating a meal at a restaurant, it will be very difficult to prove that particular establishment is to blame. He will have to prove that it was the food eaten there that caused the illness and in some cases, food poisoning can take up to seventy-two hours before the symptoms become obvious. The situation might however be different if an entire party ate a Christmas meal at a restaurant and then all went down with food poisoning.

The Food Safety Act 1990 makes it a criminal offence to sell food which is injurious to health or is not of the nature, substance or quality demanded. Doctors are under a statutory duty to inform the local health authority of any cases of food poisoning suffered by their patients. This will trigger an automatic enquiry.

## Bookings and Reservations

When someone makes a booking at a restaurant or an hotel whether in writing or by telephone, he is entering into a legally binding contract. If the customer then fails to turn up for the meal or to occupy a room, he will be in breach of that contract and the establishment may look to him to make good any losses they incur as a result. At very least it is courteous to telephone to notify a cancellation as early as possible. Most restaurateurs will be appreciative of this and not bother pursing their legal rights any further.

# 15. LEGAL RIGHTS IN RESTAURANTS

Conversely if someone books a table in a restaurant and arrives to find that there is no place for him he may be able to claim compensation for the wasted journey.

# 16. FORMS

*Form 1*: **Application for a Justices' Licence**

*To: The Clerk to the Licensing Justices for the Licensing District of [insert]*

*To: The Chief Constable of*

*To: the Proper Officer of the District Council for the district of*

*To:                         acting as Fire Authority for the area*

*TAKE NOTICE that I [insert name] of [address] in the County of [insert], who has, during the past six months carried on the trade or calling of [insert occupation], intend to apply at the licensing sessions to be held at [insert] on the     day of     19 at [time] for the grant to me of a new justices' licence authorising me to sell intoxicating liquor of all descriptions by retail for consumption either on or off the premises situate at [address of premises] and known as [name of premises]. A plan of the said premises has been deposited with the Clerk to the Justices with this Notice. The owner of the said premises is [name and address of owner].*

*Dated this     day of     19*

*Form 2*: **Certificate of Service**

*I [insert full name] [occupation] certify that on [date] 19 I did serve the persons set out in the Schedule hereto with a copy of the application for a transfer of a Justices' Licence a copy of which is annexed hereto by posting a copy of the said application to each of* the said persons at the address stated in the Schedule by recorded first class pre-paid post.

Schedule:

*[Name]*
*[Address]*

*[Name]*
*[Address]*

## Form 3: Newspaper Notice

LICENSING ACT 1964
NOTICE OF APPLICATION FOR A NEW JUSTICES' LICENCE

*In the matter of the Licensing Act 1964 we/I [insert name(s)] now residing at [insert address(es)] the Applicants, having during the past six months carried on the trade or calling of [insert] HEREBY GIVE NOTICE that it is my/our intention to apply at the licensing sessions for the licensing district of [insert] to be held at the magistrates' court at [insert address of court] on the [] day of         19    for the grant to me/us of a justice licence authorising me/us to sell by retail intoxicating liquor of all descriptions for consumption on and off/on/off the premises situate at [insert address of premises] and known by the sign of [insert name of premises] which premises [insert owner's name] of [insert owner's address] is the owner.*

*Signed:*
*Dated:*
*Name and address of applicant(s):*

## Form 4: Application for a Protection Order

NOTICE OF APPLICATION FOR A PROTECTION ORDER

To:     The Clerk to the Licensing Justices for the Licensing District of [insert] [insert address] sitting at [delete if not appropriate]

To:     The Chief Officer of Police [insert address]

To:     [Insert name and address of current licensee]

TAKE NOTICE that I/We [insert name(s) of [insert address(es)] having during the past six months carried on the trade or calling of [insert for both or one party] respectively hereby give notice that it is our intention to apply at the [ ] Magistrates' Court sitting at [insert address of court] in the County of [insert] on [insert date] for the grant to me/us to sell on the licensed premises situate at [insert address of premises] and known as [insert name of premises] such intoxicating liquors as are authorised to be sold by the justices' licence now held by [insert name of current licensee] to sell by retail intoxicating liquor of all descriptions to be sold either on or off [or as appropriate] the said premises.

Dated this          day of                    19

Signed:

Name(s) and address(es) of applicant(s):

Applicant(s)

## Form 5: Application to Transfer a Justices' Licence

To:     The Clerk to the Licensing Justices for the Licensing District of [insert]

# 16. FORMS

To:   The [Commissioner of Police for the City of London] [Town Clerk of the London Borough of
       [insert]     ]

To:   The Proper Officer of the [insert] District Council ]

To:   The [Proper Officer of [insert]   Parish Council ]
      [Chairman of the Parish Meeting of [insert]     ]

To:   The Proper Officer of the [insert] Town Council ]

To:   [Insert name(s) and address(es) of current licence holder(s)

I/WE [insert your name(s)]

of  [insert address(es)]

having during the past six months carried on the trade or calling of

  [insert]

**DO HEREBY GIVE NOTICE** that it is my/our intention to apply at the Licensing Sessions for the said District to be held at [insert name of court]
on the    day of    19    at  am/pm
for the transfer to me/us of the Justices' Licence for the sale of intoxicating liquor [insert which type e.g. of all descriptions] by retail for consumption [either on or] off the premises situate at [insert full name and address of premises]

and [to be] known by the sign of [insert name of premises] [now] [lately] held by [insert name(s) of current licensee(s)]

Dated this      day of                19

(signed).........................
*[Authorised agent on behalf of the]*
*Applicant*

NOTE: *This notice must be served not less than 21 days before the date of application. In calculating the number of days exclude the day of service and day of application.*

### Form 6: Application for a Supper Hours/Restaurant Certificate (Licensed Premises)

To:   The Clerk to the Licensing Justices for the Licensing District of *[insert[*

To:   The Chief Constable of *[insert]*

TAKE NOTICE *that I/We [insert name(s)] of [insert address(es)] intend to apply at the transfer sessions to be held at [insert name of court] on the          day of          19     for a certificate that the licensing justices for the said district of [insert] are satisfied that the licensed premises known as [insert name of premises] and situate at [insert address of premises] are structurally adapted and bona fide intended to be used for the purpose of habitually providing for the accommodation of persons frequenting the premises substantial refreshment to which the sale and supply of intoxicating liquor is ancillary.*

AND TAKE FURTHER NOTICE *that if such certificate is granted both paragraphs of section 68 of the Licensing Act 1964 will apply to the said premises from the [insert appropriate date].*

Dated this          day of          19

*(Signed)......................*

## 16. FORMS

*Applicant*

*Note:* Section 68 of the Licensing Act 1964 deals with the extension of permitted licensing hours as detailed above.

### Form 7: Application for a Special Hours Certificate

To:   The Clerk to the Licensing Justices for the Licensing District
of

TAKE NOTICE that I/We *[insert name(s)]* of *[insert address(es)]* intend to apply to the said Licensing Justices at the transfer sessions to be held on *[insert date and time]* at *[insert address of court]* for a special hours certificate under section 77 of the Licensing Act 1964 for the part mentioned below of the licensed premises situate at *[insert address of premises]* and known as *[insert name of premises]*

AND FURTHER TAKE NOTICE that if such a certificate is granted section 76 of the said Act will apply to the said part from the *[insert appropriate date]*

Dated this         day of              19

(Signed)..........................
Applicant

*Note:* Section 76 deals with permitted licensing hours where a special hours certificate is in force.

## THE LICENSING HANDBOOK

*Form 8:* **Application for Occasional Licence/Special Order of Exemption**

To:   The Clerk to the Justices for the Licensing Division of *[insert]*

To: The Chief Officer of Police for the Licensing Division of *[insert]*

I *[insert full name]*..........................................................................

of *[name & address of licensed premises or club]*............................

..............................................................................................................

.................................................*Tel. No*................................................

intend to apply to the magistrates court at *[insert address]*..............................

on *[date] [do not complete if postal application]*...............................

| Day & Date of Function | Hours required From | | To | Function ends at | Nature of function | Venue (if an occasional licence) |
|---|---|---|---|---|---|---|
| | | | | | | |

Application (s) granted as applied for above

# 16. FORMS

licence applications only )

Clerk of the Court
( Please insert address to which should be sent (postal

## Form 9: Application for a Betting Office Licence

*To:* The Clerk to the Betting Licensing Committee for [insert] in the County of [insert]

*I [insert name] of [insert address] (duly authorised in that behalf by [insert name of bookmakers]) hereby apply for and on behalf of the said Company for a betting office licence in respect of the shop premises situated at [insert address], a plan sufficient to show the layout and location of the said premises and the means of access thereto is appended hereto, and declare as follows:*
That the said Company is the holder of a bookmakers permit last renewed on the     day of        19 by [insert appropriate authority]
Dated this      day of      19

Signed:......................................................
*(Company Secretary)*
*[Company address]*

## Form 10: Application for the Renewal of a Betting Office Licence

*To:* The Clerk to the Betting Licensing Committee for the Petty Sessional Division of [insert] in the County of [insert]

*I [insert name] (duly authorised in that behalf by [insert name of company]) hereby apply for and on behalf of the said Company for the renewal of the betting office licence in respect of the betting*

*office premises situated at [insert address] aforesaid last renewed on the      day of           19 and declare as follows:*
(a) That the said Company is the holder of a bookmaker's permit last renewed on the      day of          19 by [insert appropriate authority];
(b) That there has been no change in the layout of the said premises and the means of access thereto since the last renewal of the said licence.

Dated  this    day of           19

Signed.....................................................
[Insert name]
Company Secretary
[Insert company name]

## Form 11: Application for a Bingo Licence

To:    The Clerk to the Gaming Licensing Committee for the Petty Sessions area of [insert] in the County of [insert]

[Insert name of company] of [insert company address] hereby applies for a licence under the Gaming Act 1968 in respect of the premises shown on the plan attached hereto and [if altering insert description of previous use for premises such as old Co-op supermarket etc.] [formerly known as] [insert as appropriate], situated at [insert address] aforesaid.

The premises are intended to be used for the purposes of the club named as follows: [insert name of intended club] whose principal purpose is intended to be the playing of bingo.

It is intended that the licence should be granted subject to the following restrictions under paragraphs 24 and 25 of Schedule 2 to the Act:

- to hours of gaming [insert as required]

- as to parts of the premises to be used for gaming *[insert as required]*
- as to the kinds of games to be played (apart from slot machines and gaming for small prizes): Bingo only

*If this application is granted it is desired that a direction should be given under Section 32 of the Act that the maximum number of machines (to which Part III of the Act applies) available for gaming shall be [insert a number more than 2]. The names and addresses of the Directors and Secretary of the applicant company are: [insert list]*

*A copy of the relevant certificate of consent issued by the Gaming Board of Great Britain dated the     day of       19 and numbered is attached. It is limited to a bingo club licence.*

Dated this     day of       19

Signed:................................................
*[Insert name of signatory]*
*[Insert position in company]*
*[Insert company address]*

# 17. GLOSSARY

*Betting Agency Permit*: A permit which allows a person to hold a betting office licence.
*Betting Office Licence*: A licence permitting the running of a betting office.
*Bingo Licence*: A licence permitting the playing of bingo.
*Bookmakers' Permit*: A permit which allows a person to carry on business as a book maker.
*Brewster Sessions*: Magistrates' annual licensing meetings.
*Certificate of Service*: A certificate showing that documents have been properly served.
*Children's Certificate*: A certificate which allows children under the age of fourteen years to enter a bar when accompanied by an adult.
*Extended Hours Order*: An order extending licensing hours for live entertainment where premises hold a supper hours certificate *(q.v.)*.
*Gaming Licence*: A licence permitting gaming on licensed or registered premises.
*General Orders of Exemption*: Orders which permanently extend licensing hours to cater for a particular group of people.
*Licensing Hours*: Period of time in which the sale of alcohol is permitted.
*Occasional Licence*: A licence allowing alcohol to be served at a place other than at the licensed premises.
*Occasional Permission*: An order allowing organisations to sell alcohol at functions which are related to their business or trade.
*Off Licence*: A licence permitting the sale of alcohol for consumption away from the premises.
*On Licence*: A licence permitting the sale and consumption of alcohol on the premises.
*Ordinary Removal*: A transfer of a licence from one set of premises to another. Circumstances will dictate whether the removal is ordinary or special *(q.v.)*
*Part IV Licence*: General term covering restaurant and residential licences.

# 17. GLOSSARY

*Performing Rights Society Licence*: A licence protecting the copyright of a composer or publisher when recorded music is played in public.

*Phonographic Performance Limited Licence*: A licence protecting the copyright of a record company or producer when recorded music is played in public.

*Protection Order*: An order protecting the seller of alcohol from prosecution until a licence has been transferred to him.

*Public Entertainment Licence*: Licences granted by the local authority to permit music and dancing on approved premises.

*Registration Certificate*: A certificate under which clubs are permitted to sell alcohol or allow gaming on their premises

*Residential Licence*: A licence allowing the sale and supply of alcohol to people staying at residential establishments and to their guests.

*Restaurant Certificate*: The same as a supper hours certificate (*q.v.*)

*Restaurant Licence*: A licence allowing alcohol to be served to diners only as an accompaniment to a meal.

*Section 34 Licence*: A fruit machine licence.

*Section 77 Licence*: A nightclub licence.

*Special Hours Certificate*: A certificate permitting the extension of licensing hours to 2am or later where the premises are licensed for music and dancing and serve food. This is referred to as a section 77 licence (*q.v.*) in nightclub applications.

*Special Orders of Exemption*: An order extending licensing hours for one off occasions for clubs and licensed premises.

*Supper Hours Certificate*: A certificate extending licensing hours for one hour in the evening and in the "gap" in hours on Xmas Day for premises serving meals. Also known as a restaurant certificate.

*Special Removals*: See ordinary removals (*q.v.*).

*Transfer Sessions*: Four sessions held by the licensing justices during the year to which most licensing applications are made.

# 18. FURTHER READING

## Statutes

Licensing law derives almost entirely from Acts of Parliament. The most important in respect of liquor licensing are the Licensing Act 1964, the Licensing Act 1988 and the Licensing (Sunday Hours) Act 1995. The Gaming Act 1988 and The Marriage Act 1994 are equally important in their own fields. It is possible, but not generally very helpful, to consult these statutes in the form they are published by the HMSO. Similarly there are a large number of statutory instruments, dealing largely with procedural matters, introduced by Ministers acting under the authority given to them by Acts of Parliament.

## Legal Textbooks

The leading textbook on licensing is *Paterson's Licensing Acts*. Published annually this is considered the bible of licensing by lawyers and justices' clerks. It contains all the statutory material which relate to liquor and gaming licensing, though for the moment at least marriage venues remain outside its ambit. The statutes contain annotation in the form of footnotes. While easier to read than the raw statutes, it is still not a book that a layperson will find particularly comprehensible, nor at over £130 wish to buy!

Nearly as comprehensive a guide to licensing statutes is *Stone's Justices' Manual*. this three volume work contains virtually all the law that magistrates courts might find themselves dealing with. It devotes several hundred pages to licences. It is stocked in most public libraries, but its format is similar to *Paterson's*.

Although written primarily with lawyers in mind, *Underhills' Licensing Guide* by Simon Mehigan and Lawrence Stevens the 12th edition of which was published in 1996 is considerably easier to use.

# 18. FURTHER READING

By far the best guide to gaming law is *Smith & Monkham's Law of Betting, Gaming and Lotteries*. Originally published in 1987 it is regularly updated by looseleaf supplements.

## Other Helpful Publications

There are also a number of books, written primarily for the layperson, which deal with licensing. These include the BBC's *Watchdog Guide to Getting a Better Deal* by David Berry last published in 1994, the *Good Housekeeping Consumer Guides: You and Your Rights* by Suzanne Wilkinson and Patricia Schofield, 1995.

On public entertainment licences, the leaflets produced by the Performing Rights Society and Phonographic Performance Limited are both useful and free.

# INDEX

betting office licence 80
  application for 81
  appeal 83
  death of holder 85
  notices 81
  refusal of 82
  renewal 84
betting agency permits 80
Betting Licensing Committee 80
bingo 100
bookmakers' permits 80
Brewster Sessions 14, 48

case histories
  marriage licence 73-74
  off licence 25-30
  protection order 31-35
  public entertainment licence 76
  restaurant licence 54-55
  transfer of justices licence 30
certificate of service 22, 32
children 17
children's certificates 17
clerk to the justices 21, 22
clubs 56-67
  appeals 63
  application for registration certificate 56
  extended hours order 57
  objections 59-60
  permitted hours 55
  registration certificate 56-58

restaurant certificate 55
  special hours certificate 56
  supper hours certificate 55
copyright music 75

drinking up time 19, 40, 43

Food Safety Act 1990 108
fruit machine licence 99

Gaming Act 1968 86, 87, 89, 91, 92, 96, 97 100, 102, 103, 104
Gaming Board 86, 87, 91, 92, 93
Gaming Clubs (Permitted Areas) Regulations 1971 91
gaming licence 86
  appeal 92-93
  application for 86-87, 88
  cancellation of 94-95
  companies 99
  consent application 87
  convictions 83
  death of licence holder 97
  disqualification 96
  fees 98
  notices 88
  refusing to grant 90-91
  refusing to transfer 98
  relinquishing 99
  renewal of 93
  restrictions 91-92

# INDEX

restrictions on games 92
revocation 93-94
transfer of 97-98
gaming licence (members clubs) 101
   appeal 102
   application for 101
   cancellation of registration 103
   refusing to grant 101
   registration certificates 104
   relinquishing registration 104
   restrictions on games 104
garages 16-17

hotels 16

justices licences 14-15
   application for 21
   convictions of holder 17
   disqualification from holding 17
   duration of 14
   forfeiture 49-50
   new licences 19
   off licence 15
   on licence 15
   Part IV licences
      see *restaurant licences*
   restrictions on
      persons 17
      premises 16-17
   revocation 49-50
   surrender of 50
   suspension of 51-51
      transfer of licence
         persons 33-34
         premises 35-36

licences
   beerhouse 49
   betting office 80
   bingo 100
   civil marriage 59
   combined restaurant & residential 52
   early closing 44
   fruit machine 99
   gaming 86
   nightclub 77
   occasional 45
   on 15
   off 15
   Part IV
      see *restaurant*
   Phonographic Performance 78
   public entertainment 75
   public performance 76
   residential 52
   restaurant 52
   seasonal 44
licences in suspense 51-52
Licensing Act 1964 14, 115, 18, 44, 52
Licensing Act 1988 18
Licensing (Sunday Hours) Act 1995 14, 18
licensing hours 18-19
   extension of 34
   restrictions on 19, 39
   variations to 34
licensing justices 14
licensing of marriage venues 68
   application for 68
   conditions 71
   fees 70

notices 71
records kept 73
registrars 70
religious connections 70
renewal of 72
review of 73
revocation of 72
room 72

Marriage Act 1994 70
members clubs
  see *gaming licences (members clubs)*

nightclubs 66-67

occasional permission 46-47
orders of exemption 35-39
  general 38-39
  special 39
ordinary removal 36

Part IV licence
  see *restaurant licence*
Performing Rights Society 76-77
  fees 77-78
Phonographic Performance Limited 78-79
protection order 31-32
public entertainment licence 75

register of justices licences 20
restaurant certificate 39
restaurants 106
  bookings & reservations 108-09
  complaints 107, 108

food 106
hygiene 108
restaurant licences 52

sale by retail 15, 16
special removal 36

underage drinking 28, 29
undertakings 25, 29, 35

variations to licensing hours 38
  extended hours order 42-43
  notices 44
  orders of exemption 38

# Also from Fitzwarren Handbooks

### *The Landlords' & Tenants' Handbook*
Alan Matthews
A practical guide to renting property, looking at the potential pitfalls from both the landlords' and the tenants' point of view.

### *The Litigation Handbook*
Alan Matthews
A concise account of how the English civil courts operate. Contains sufficient information to enable anyone to pursue or defend a simple claim in the county court.

### *The Elections Handbook*
Ron Kendall
An account of the procedures that are used in United Kingdom elections. An invaluable guide for anyone running for public office and for electoral staff.

### *The Employment Handbook*
Martin Hannibal and Steven Hardy
A guide to the legal side of the employment relationship. Contains the information employers and employees need to know to be able to resolve most of the scrapes they may find themselves in.

### *The Family and Divorce Handbook*
Lindsey Mendoza
A compassionate and informed guide to dealing with the legal problems, relating particularly to money and children, that inevitably arise when a marriage breaks down.

Fitzwarren Handbooks endeavour to provide clear and practical explanations of matters that have a legal flavour, in such a way as to be accessible to laypeople, while still providing sufficient depth to be of assistance to lawyers and other professionals working in the relevant areas.